RESEARCH ON
PSYCHOANALYTIC PSYCHOTHERAPY
WITH ADULTS

The EFPP Series

Editor-in-Chief: *John Tsiantis*
Associate Editors: *Brian Martindale* (Adult Section)
                    Didier Houzel (Child & Adolescent Section)
                    Alessandro Bruni (Group Section)

OTHER TITLES IN THE SERIES

Research on Psychoanalytic Psychotherapy with Adults

Edited by

*Phil Richardson, Horst Kächele,
Camilla Renlund*

Foreword by
Peter Fonagy

published by

KARNAC

for

The European Federation
for Psychoanalytic Psychotherapy
in the Public Health Services

First published in 2004 by
H. Karnac (Books) Ltd.
6 Pembroke Buildings, London NW10 6RE

British Library Cataloguing in Publication Data

A C.I.P. for this book is available from the British Library

ISBN: 1-85575-949-7

10 9 8 7 6 5 4 3 2 1

Edited, designed, and produced by Communication Crafts

Printed in Great Britain

www.karnacbooks.com

for Irène

CONTENTS

ABOUT THE AUTHORS

ANTHONY W. BATEMAN (United Kingdom) is Consultant Psychiatrist in Psychotherapy at Barnet, Enfield, & Haringey Mental Health Trust; and Honorary Senior Lecturer at University College and Royal Free Medical Schools. His special interest is the treatment of personality disorders.

PETER FONAGY, PhD, FBA (United Kingdom), is Freud Memorial Professor of Psychoanalysis and Director of the Sub-Department of Clinical Health Psychology at University College London; Director of the Child and Family Centre at the Menninger Foundation, Kansas; and Director of Research at the Anna Freud Centre, London. He is a clinical psychologist and training and supervising analyst in the British Psycho-Analytical Society in child and adult analysis. He chairs the Research Committee of the International Psychoanalytic Association and is a Fellow of the British Academy.

INES GITZINGER, PhD (Germany), is a clinical psychologist and adult (and child) psychoanalyst working in Freiburg. She was trained in adolescent psychoanalysis at the University of Ulm. She is a member of DGPT, the Committee of the German Association of Adolescent Psychoanalytic Psychotherapy and Psychosomatics.

RALF GRABHORN, MD (Germany), is a specialist in psychotherapeutic medicine. He is Assistant Medical Director of the Department of Psychosomatic Medicine, Hospital of the Johann Wolfgang Goethe University in Frankfurt. His main research fields are eating disorders, inpatient psychotherapeutic treatment, and qualitative and quantitative methods.

TILMAN GRANDE, PhD (Germany), is a clinical psychologist, psychoanalyst, and the senior researcher at the Department of Psychosomatics at the University of Heidelberg. His main foci of research are psychodynamic diagnostics, psychotherapeutic process, and structural change in psychoanalysis.

JOHAN GRANT [formerly BLOMBERG], PhD (Sweden), is a licensed psychologist, and he has a doctorate in psychology from Linköping University. He was the manager of data collection and data analysis of the Stockholm Outcome of Psychotherapy and Psychoanalysis Project and is currently active as a self-employed organizational development consultant in Stockholm.

DOROTHEA HUBER, MD, PhD (Germany), is a psychoanalyst (DPG) and Assistant Medical Director at the Institute and Outpatient Clinic of Psychosomatic Medicine, Klinikum rechts der Isar, University of München (Munich)

BURKARD JÄGER, PhD (Germany), works as research fellow at the Hannover Medical School. He is trained in psychoanalytically oriented, behavioural, and group psychotherapy. He is engaged in training in psychotherapy and supervision. Further areas of special interest are psychotherapy research concerning eating disorders and coping strategies with tinnitus.

THORSTEN JAKOBSEN (Germany) is a psychologist, psychoanalyst in practice, and researcher at the Department of Psychosomatics at the University of Heidelberg. His main foci of research are statistics, psychotherapy research, and quality management in psychotherapy.

HORST KÄCHELE, MD (Germany), is a specialist in psychotherapeutic medicine and a psychoanalyst (IPA). He is full professor and Chair of the Department of Psychotherapy and Psychosomatic Medicine at Ulm University; he also directs the Centre for Psychotherapy Research in Stuttgart. He is a member of the Society for Psychotherapy Research. His main research fields are psychoanalytic process and outcome research, psychosocial issues of bone marrow transplantation, and the treatment of eating disorders.

WOLFRAM KELLER, MD (Germany), is a training psychoanalyst, internist, and the head of the Theodor-Wenzel Hospital, Department of Internal Medicine and Psychosomatics. His focus of research is outcome in psychoanalysis and psychotherapy, psychosomatic diseases, and quality management in psychotherapy.

GUENTHER KLUG, MD (Germany), is a psychoanalyst and Assistant Medical Director at the Municipal Hospital of Munich-Harlaching, Department for Psychosomatic Diseases and Psychotherapy.

PETER KÖHLER (Germany) is a clinical psychologist trained in behavioural therapies. He has been a staff member of the Department of Psychosomatic Medicine of the Medical University of Lübeck, Germany, and has undertaken research on eating disorders. He now works in the Holstein-Clinic, a hospital for alcohol addicts, and in a private psychotherapeutic practice.

WERNER KÖPP, MD (Germany), is an internist and psychoanalyst, assistant professor, and a member of the medical faculty of the Free University of Berlin, and a member of the German Psychoanalytic Society (DPG). He is the author of several papers about eating disorders, and he received the Christina Barz award for his research in the year 2000.

PETER MALEWSKI, PhD (Germany), works as research fellow at the Hanover Medical School. He is engaged in psychotherapy research, mainly on the methods and statistics of a variety of different studies.

KINGSLEY NORTON (United Kingdom) is a consultant psychotherapist and Director of Henderson Hospital, Surrey. He is also a reader in psychotherapy at St George's Hospital Medical School, London University, and a former professional member of the Society of Analytical Psychologists, London.

CLAUDIA OBERBRACHT (Germany) is a psychologist, psychoanalyst, and researcher at the Department of Psychosomatics at the University of Heidelberg. Her main foci of research are psychic structure and outcome in psychoanalysis and psychotherapy.

CAMILLA RENLUND (Finland) is an adult psychiatrist and a member of the research team of the Helsinki Psychotherapy Study, a randomized psychotherapy outcome study. She also works as a psychoanalyst in private practice in Helsinki and is an associate member of the Finnish Psycho-Analytical Society.

PHIL RICHARDSON (United Kingdom) is a clinical psychologist and qualified as a psychoanalyst with the British Psychoanalytical Society. He is professor of clinical psychology at the University of Essex and Head of Psychology at the Tavistock & Portman NHS Trust, where he is also Director of the Psychotherapy Evaluation Research Unit. He is currently Editor of *Psychology and Psychotherapy: Theory, Research and Practice* (formerly the *British Journal of Medical Psychology*).

GERD RUDOLF, MD (Germany), is a psychiatrist, a psychoanalyst, and the head of the Department of Psychosomatics at the University of Heidelberg. He has developed a concept of psychic structure and done empirical research on structural change in psychodynamic psychotherapies.

ROLF SANDELL (Sweden) is Professor of Clinical Psychology at Linköping University and is a member of the Swedish Psychoanalytic Society. He is the Director of the Stockholm Outcome of Psychotherapy and Psychoanalysis Project and currently has several other ongoing research projects in psychotherapy and psychological treatment.

SILKE SCHMIDT, PhD (Germany), is a psychologist, now at the Department of Medical Psychology at the University Hospital Hamburg-Eppendorf. Her main research field is the clinical application of attachment theory related to coping with medical disorders.

BERNHARD STRAUSS, PhD (Germany), is professor of medical psychology and a psychoanalyst. He is the Head of the Department of Medical Psychology at the University Hospital of the Friedrich-Schiller University at Jena (Thuringia). Currently he is President of the German College of Psychosomatic Medicine.

JÖRN VON WIETERSHEIM, PhD (Germany), clinical psychologist, is professor for psychosomatic medicine in the Department of Psychotherapy and Psychosomatic Medicine at the University of Ulm, Germany. He is the head of the day treatment and the outpatient units in this department. His main research fields are eating disorders, chronic inflammatory bowel diseases, and psychotherapeutic process and outcome studies.

FIONA WARREN, MA (United Kingdom), is a psychologist in research at Henderson Hospital therapeutic community and St. George's Hospital Medical School in South London. She was an author of the successful bid to the UK Department of Health to replicate Henderson Hospital in two new sites and a member of the Steering Group for this unique service development. She is Chair of the Research Subgroup for this new national service. Her research interests are in personality disorders, self-harming behaviours, and treatment and research methods in the evaluation of psychological health care.

ABBREVIATIONS AND ACRONYMS

ANOVA	Analysis of variance
APES	Assimilation of Problematic Experiences Scale
BADO	Basic Documentation of the German College of Psychosomatic Medicine
BDI	Beck Depression Inventory
BMI	body-mass index
BPD	borderline personality disorder
BSI	Borderline Syndrome Index
BSS	Symptom Severity Score
CPN	Community Psychiatric Nurse
DBT	Dialectical Behaviour Therapy
DGPT	Deutsche Gesellschaft für Psychoanalyse, Psychotherapie, Psychosomatik und Tiefenpsychologie [German Association of Adolescent Psychoanalytic Psychotherapy and Psychosomatics]
DIB	Diagnostic Interview for Borderlines
DSM	Diagnostic and Statistical Manual of Mental Disorders
EBM	evidence-based medicine
ECR	extra-contractual referrals
EDI	Eating Disorders Inventory
FKBS	Questionnaire for Coping Strategies
FLZ	Life Satisfaction Questionnaire
FPI	*Freiburger Persönlichkeitsinventar* [Freiburg Personality Inventory]
FPI–R	Freiburg Personality Inventory, revised version
GAF	Global Assessment of Functioning
GAS	Goal Attainment Scaling
GP	general practitioner
GSI	Global Severity Index
HAMD	Hamilton Depression Scale
HAQ	Helping Alliance Questionnaire
HRSD	Hamilton Rating Scale for Depression

HSCS	Heidelberg Structural Change Scale
ICC	Intra Class Correlation Coefficient
ICD	*International Classification of Diseases*
ICD–10	*International Classification of Diseases*
IDA	Irritability, Depression and Anxiety Scale
IDCL	International Diagnostic Checklist for ICD–10 and DSM–IV
IIP	Inventory of Interpersonal Problems
IIP–C	Inventory of Interpersonal Problems, short
IIP–D	Inventory of Interpersonal Problems, German version
INTREX	Introject questionnaire
iTAB	Initial Working Alliance
MMPI	Minnesota Multiphasic Inventory
MPS	Munich Psychotherapy Study
MZ–ESS	Multi-Centre Eating Disorders Questionnaire
NIMH	National Institutes of Mental Health
OPD	Operationalized Psychodynamic Diagnosis
PA	psychoanalysis
PD	personality disorder
PDQ–R	Personality Disorder Questionnaire
PRP	Psychotherapy Research Project
PSKB–Se	Psychic and Social-Communicative Questionnaire
PT	psychodynamic psychotherapy
P–T–O	Problem–Treatment–Outcome
RCT	randomized controlled trial
RHA	Regional Health Authority
RMP	Relationship Management Psychotherapy
RSE	Rosenberg Self-Esteem Scale
SASB	Structural Analysis of Social Behaviour
SCID–II	Structured Clinical Interview for the DSM–III–R
SCL	Symptom Checklist
SG Scale	Health Scale of the TPF
SOZU	Social Support Questionnaire
SPC	Scales of Psychological Capacities
SPR	Society for Psychotherapy Research
STOPP	Stockholm Outcome of Psychotherapy and Psychoanalysis
TAB	Therapeutic Working Alliance
TASC	Therapeutic Attitudes Scale
TC	therapeutic community
ThId	Therapeutic Identity
TPF	Trierer Persönlichkeitsfragebogen (Personality Questionnaire)
TR-EAT	German Multi-centre Eating Disorder Study
VEV	Veränderungs Fragebogen des Erlebens und Verhaltens (Change in Experiencing and Behaviour Questionnaire)
WbQ	Well-being Questionnaire

T he present volume is the seventh in the EFPP/Karnac Clinical Monograph Series, the first of which appeared in 1995. It is the first devoted specifically to research in adult psychoanalytic psychotherapy and represents a collaborative effort by editors and authors from Germany, the United Kingdom, Finland, and Sweden. As such, it reflects the global aims of the European Federation of Psychoanalytic Psychotherapy in the Public Sector in contributing to the development of a pan-European community of psychoanalytic psychotherapists. Further monographs are planned under the overall guiding editorship of Professor John Tsiantis, the Chief Editor of the Series. These will focus on psychoanalytic psychotherapy research with children and on therapist issues in the processes and outcomes of psychoanalytic psychotherapy. Interested readers should visit the EFPP website at www.efpp.org.

In the present-day culture of evidence-based practice as a guiding principle for the delivery of public- and private-sector health services, the critical importance of collating empirical research findings relating to psychoanalytic psychotherapy cannot be overstated. Evidence-based clinical guidelines are increasingly finding their way into the mental health arena (see, for example, *Treatment Choice in Psychological Therapies and Counselling*: Department of Health, 2001), and, as of yet, the place of psychoanalytic psychotherapy within such guidelines is far from extensive. The present monograph brings together a number of research reports and overviews, all of which have used conventional empirical research methodologies and illustrate, we believe, the potential of such methods to explore questions of real significance to psychoanalytic psychotherapists throughout Europe. Peter Fonagy's excellent Foreword locates the studies within an overview of the contemporary research context.

We are indebted to the Series Editors John Tsiantis (Chief Editor) and Brian Martindale (Associate Editor for the Individual Psychoanalytic Psychotherapy Section of EFPP) for their patient and helpful guidance in the production of this monograph. We also wish to thank Amaryllis Holland for her editorial acumen in the proofreading of the individual chapters, as well as Beverley Foster-Davis and Sharon Novara for additional editorial support.

Phil Richardson, Horst Kächele, & Camilla Renlund

FOREWORD

Peter Fonagy

Psychoanalysis has not fared well in the era of evidence-based medicine (EBM) (Sackett, Rosenberg, Gray, Haynes, & Richardson, 1996). While the United Kingdom and all countries of continental Europe are forced to rationalize healthcare costs to a greater or lesser extent, few general principles have emerged to offer reasonable and ethical grounds for such rationalization (Knapp, 1997). Arguably, as a consequence, the availability of sound empirical research findings to support the provision of particular treatments has become a requirement of statutory funding, in psychiatry as in other specialities. There can be no doubt that the provision of services on the basis of evidence of effectiveness is preferable to service distribution based on postcodes or luck. Nevertheless, there is quite a high price to pay for equity.

Not surprisingly, expensive long-term treatments like psychoanalytic therapy have quickly fallen victim to EBM-orientated criteria (Westen & Morrison, 2001). Evidence for the effectiveness of psychoanalytic therapy is lacking. Why? Short-term treatments are undoubtedly easier to research using random assignments for both practical and ethical reasons. At a more impressionistic level, we might say that the world-view that is normally created by working intensively and on a long-term basis with individuals suffering from relatively enduring and severe mental disorders is incompatible with the ethos of tightly controlled investigations of efficacy. Those who work at close quarters with the human mind will inevitably have an impression of reductionism when they see the full complexity of an individual's struggle with internal and external experience reduced to a single hundred-point scale (Endicott,

Spitzer, Heiss, & Cohen, 1976; Shaffer et al., 1983) or even 12 five-point ones (Wing, Curtis, & Beevor, 1996; Wing, Lelliott, & Beevor, 2000). On top of that, even the anchor points are badly defined. Moreover, the spirit of late-twentieth-century pragmatism and utilitarianism, perhaps by analogy with the remarkable technological advances of this period, often equated the novel with the good and the traditional with the outdated (Giddens, 1999). The rapid progress of technology and biological science has held out the possibility of biochemical rehabilitation, which, many continue to feel, offers the only viable solution to the challenge of treating mental disorder. This is already a toxic mixture for psychoanalytic thinking, but add the history of the unashamed arrogance of many of our psychodynamic colleagues, who until recently have all too frequently treated their non-psychoanalytically trained mental health worker colleagues with, at best, benevolent tolerance and, at worst, contempt and disdain, and you have the complete background to the current crisis for psychoanalytically orientated psychotherapies.

To take but one example from the United States, where the crisis was first to come to a head:

> Although long-term, so-called intensive therapy has been dying for years, some of our profession's leaders cling fiercely to the illusion that it works and that only psychiatrists can do it. However, since we have proof only of its high cost and not its effectiveness, psychiatry's reluctance to admit that the emperor is indeed naked only increases public scepticism. [Detre & McDonald, 1997, p. 203]

The hostility towards psychoanalytic ideas that currently dominates the United States may have its historical origins in the fierce competition for power and control between biological psychiatry and psychoanalysis in U.S. medical schools (Cooper, 1996; Michels, 1994). It is hard to envisage such a titanic struggle in a European context, where psychoanalysis has never fully dominated the health-care system. Limited versions of the same conflicts are, however, evident (Chiesa & Fonagy, 1999). While half a century ago psychoanalysis could credibly present itself as the sole form of humane mental health care (Menninger, Mayman, & Pruyser,

1963), current alternatives to psychoanalytic therapy are mostly relatively sophisticated, well-structured, and by no means mindless interventions. Cognitive behaviour therapy and psycho-pharmacological treatments have powerful effects and are reasonably well tolerated by users.

Across Europe, expert groups in many countries are busy surveying the literature in sincere attempts to identify the treatments that may be most helpful for their citizens who suffer from enduring mental disorder (e.g. Department of Health, 1995; Health Council of the Netherlands, 2001; Weisz, Hawley, Pilkonis, Woody, & Follette, 2000). Statutory funding for psychological therapy is threatened in many countries by the readiness with which pharmacological treatments can be made available to relatively large groups. Popular views concerning the causes of mental illness have changed during "the decade of the brain", in many places powerfully supported by far-sighted pharmaceutical companies, to the point where commonly held theories of psychological disorder have shifted towards the constitutional and antidepressants are, bizarrely, accepted as appropriate means of addressing social difficulties (Cornwell, 1996). Behaviour genetics research has not helped (Fonagy, in press). The limited range of environments sampled by most studies and the tendency to conflate error variance with non-shared environment have combined to undermine psychodynamic claims concerning the causal significance of shared early family environment, the bread and butter of psychotherapeutic narrative (Rutter, 2000).

All this is not to say that every recent development has been inconsistent with a psychoanalytic understanding. For example, few now believe that severe psychological disorders are episodic conditions that can be addressed in the long term by a short-term intervention. Problems persist after brief interventions have done their best (e.g. Shea et al., 1992). There has been a backlash against the reification of findings from randomized controlled trials, particularly the limitation on the generalizability of findings emerging from very tightly controlled investigations (Markowitz & Street, 1999; Weisz & Jensen, 1999). There has been a heartfelt outcry for effectiveness rather than efficacy research, the former ostensibly creating a more truthful representation of the value of a treatment in the field (Wells, 1999). There has been a resurgence of interest in qualitative as opposed to quantitative data gathering (e.g. Mayes & Pope, 2000), and so-called expert groups who have generated prescriptive lists of approved therapies have come under occasionally severe criticism (Weisz, Hawley, Pilkonis, Woody, & Follette, 2000). Sometimes brain research has been successfully introduced to advance the psychodynamic cause, with studies providing striking support for classical ideas receiving quite extensive coverage (Solms, 2000; Solms & Nersessian, 1999). Perhaps even more important have been related social initiatives based on the assumption of "developmental programming", early influences bringing about enduring change in neural structure and function (Hertzman & Wiens, 1996). The empirical literature on the long-term and trans-generational effects of quality of parent–infant attachment has also helped to make psychoanalytic concerns with infancy more plausible (O'Connor, Bredenkamp, Rutter, & the English and Romanian Adoptees Study Team, 1999; O'Connor, Rutter, & the English and Romanian Adoptees Study Team, 2000). User-led research exploring the strategies of individuals living and coping with mental distress also stresses familiar dynamic themes such as the importance of relationships with family and friends, self-esteem drawn from peer groups, and respectful treatment by professionals (Faulkner, 2000; Rose, 2001). Nonetheless, these and other developments have done little to reverse the underlying trend away from long-term psychodynamic therapies towards long-term pharmacological or short-term psychological (usually cognitive–behavioural) treatments.

To counteract these trends, three developments to the currently dominant knowledge base will be necessary. First, we require evidence concerning the *specific patient groups* who uniquely benefit from psychoanalytic interventions and, related to this, assessment systems that help to identify these individuals, either in terms of diagnosis and symptomatology or in terms of characteristic modes of mental functioning or even social conditions. Second, we need *sensitive measurement systems* that identify changes in psychological functioning associated with long-term psychoanalytic therapy that may go beyond symptomatic improvement and indicate benefits that are either valued by clients (or carers) or can be shown to be predictive of relative freedom from future difficulties (prevention).

Third, we need to develop new *adaptations of psychoanalytic therapy* that extend and improve upon existing applications to increase their generalizability across clinical groups and enhance their impact in terms of either symptom relief or prevention.

The contributors to the present volume have all, in their own ways, advanced one or more of the above goals. An excellent, well-controlled study attempting to address the first of these three aims comes from Horst Kächele's laboratory in Ulm. Kächele is a key figure in empirical psychoanalysis, bringing infectious enthusiasm mixed with an iconoclastic approach to his subject. The large-scale eating disorder study attempted to identify which patients with eating disorder problems were particularly well suited to a psychoanalytic approach in inpatient treatment. While a clearly identifiable group benefited remarkably from the treatment they were offered, their success could not be predicted by a traditional questionnaire measure of personality. Perhaps a new approach to measurement of individual differences is required by psychoanalytic investigations.

A suggestion about a possible direction for such a project is provided by the programme of work on inpatient psychotherapy reported from the University of Jena. Bernhard Strauss and colleagues looked at the Inventory of Interpersonal Problems (IIP) as a predictor of therapeutic benefit. They report that psychodynamic treatment may be, somewhat paradoxically, most appropriate for patients who report a wider variety and severity of interpersonal problems. This may be linked to the fundamentally interpersonal focus of modern psychoanalytic therapy. The greater benefit of those with high IIP scores is most probably accounted for by the assumption that those who have the greatest awareness of their interpersonal problems are most likely to benefit from a treatment that has interpersonal understanding as its core aim. It is hard to know from a psychodynamic standpoint how responses from a self-report questionnaire on relationship problems might interface with the social behaviour of individuals in an inpatient group therapy setting. It seems likely that only the combination of observational and self-report measures will ultimately yield conclusive answers concerning the precise relationship of initial self-awareness and overt behaviour as predictors of responsiveness to an insight-orientated therapy.

The Heidelberg–Berlin study is an excellent example of an attempt to show that long-term intensive therapy may yield added treatment value for severe psychological difficulties when the measurement system is up to the task of showing key differences in character, including relationship patterns, conflict types, and structural capacities. The OPD (Operationalized Psychodynamic Diagnosis) system described in this chapter has become an enormously valuable addition to the empirical armamentarium of psychoanalytic clinicians (Cierpka et al., 1995). A key limitation of the field that has hindered the cumulative construction of a psychoanalytic knowledge base has been the absence of even a rudimentary classification system to describe clinical cases (Gabbard, Gunderson, & Fonagy, 2002). A similar initiative with equally great potential is the Munich Psychotherapy Project, which offers a thorough test of the Scale of Psychological Capacities (SPC) originating from the research efforts of the group around Robert Wallerstein in San Francisco. An important criterion for showing the unique contribution of psychoanalytic therapy is the demonstration of changes in the manner of psychological function that cannot be reduced to symptomatic change. As the authors of this chapter emphasize, the *prima facie* justification for such a measurement approach is clear, since psychoanalysis is the only current therapeutic intervention that does not aim at the attainment of symptomatic change. The work shows that change beyond the symptomatic may be reliably measured. What value such changes represent in terms of the depressed patient's long-term functioning remains to be established.

The Munich Psychotherapy Study is undoubtedly the most carefully conducted study to date designed to address the vexing question of how, if at all, intensive psychodynamic therapy (psychoanalysis) differs in its effects from psychodynamic psychotherapy. The study is remarkable because it uses a randomized controlled design and because all the therapists involved are highly experienced. The strength of the study, which the present contribution highlights, is the use of a measure specifically designed to identify changes that may take place in psychoanalysis but are not so characteristic of changes observed following psychoanalytic psychotherapy. The establishment of the validity of such a measure is of paramount importance. The SPCs were designed to measure structural change. The SPC is a clinician-coded measure, and thus blindness in the ratings will be very important to demonstrate. The present contribution, however, clearly establishes its relative independence from simpler measures of adaptation (GAF: Global Assessment of Functioning) as well as symptom severity. The inter-rater reliability of the measure is good, and some progress is reported towards establishing construct validity and convergent validity by showing depression-specific abnormality in the measure in a group of depressed patients and correlations with self-report measures of interpersonal functioning that might be predicted for this group. The report speaks volumes to the careful way in which this extremely important study is being conducted.

The fluidity of the current psychoanalytic research knowledge base is well illustrated by the contrary position adopted by Ralph Sandell's Karolinska Institute (STOPP) project. The Stockholm study is by far the largest of the prospective investigations of psychoanalysis reported to date. The advantage of intensive compared to non-intensive treatment was interestingly clearest in the symptomatic domain. Thus, the jury is still out on the empirical question of whether measuring change beyond symptoms (as sought by many, including the Munich group) is indeed to be the touchstone of psychoanalytic therapy research, or whether the most effective demonstrations are the simplest, and a focus on symptom measurement is sufficient. But the STOPP study also highlights the third point of our psychoanalytic trident of effectiveness research programme outlined above. The study shows that the superiority of psychoanalysis over psychotherapy, in the long term, is clearest when unmodified "classical" psychoanalytic ideas govern psychotherapeutic interventions. This approach might be almost ineffective when administered non-intensively. If the ideology of the therapist is broader, the superiority of psychoanalysis over psychotherapy is less marked. While these findings concern ideology rather than actual technique, they do highlight the need to further evolve applications of psychoanalysis, particularly since many of those trained to practice psychoanalysis now often only practice psychotherapy after qualification.

The first contribution from London, from St Anne's Hospital, is in the same spirit of broadening ideology and applications. This is a randomized controlled trial that served to advance the understanding and treatment of borderline personality disorder (BPD)—

defined psychiatrically—as well as demonstrate remarkably successful long-term outcomes. An important point to note about this study is the extensive use of nurse practitioners in this psychotherapeutic day-hospital intervention. Some years ago, these therapists might have been treated with condescension by psychoanalytically trained psychiatric colleagues. Now they represent almost the only controlled evaluation of a psychoanalytically oriented intervention with this group. The immense pragmatic importance of Anthony Bateman's work is due to his translation of basic psychoanalytic principles to enable practitioners who would be considered untrained by traditional standards to administer a systematic and powerful intervention. If psychoanalysis is going to survive in a statutory service that is distributed on a principle of equity, such an "enabling" approach must inevitably be at the core of technical adaptation.

The second contribution from London describes research on an inpatient service for a relatively dangerous group of patients, which Kingsley Norton and Bridget Dolan have directed with great effectiveness. This unit tackles some of the most difficult personality-disordered patients: young men whose psychopathology is combined with criminal tendency and significant dangerousness. The report is a case study in itself, showing how retrospective studies of outcome can develop into prospective studies as definitions of improvement are refined. An important contribution of this study is the cost-effectiveness data that the Henderson Hospital was able to compile, which undoubtedly contributed to the Henderson model being adopted in a number of other U.K. settings. Such data are not often available for psychoanalytic psychotherapy evaluations (Gabbard, Lazar, Hornberger, & Spiegel, 1997). The controlled study reported in the chapter suggests important benefits from the programme in the domains of both symptomatology and mood and underscores the value of the service in that mood variables such as irritability appear not to improve spontaneously at all; in fact, they show a slight tendency to worsen in the absence of the therapeutic community provided by the Henderson.

This is a pioneering volume of work in progress. It is important and exciting work by talented pioneers who have responded effectively to an intellectual as well as a professional call. It is clear from the variety of findings reported in this stimulating volume that

many of the traditional ideas concerning psychoanalytic psychotherapy will need to be revised. This does not signal the demise of
the psychoanalytic approach but, rather, indicates the great potential for further development of its knowledge base. In the past,
psychoanalysis as a theory has not benefited markedly from the
rapid virtuous cycle of theoretical development leading to increasingly refined observation and data collection, which, in turn, produces findings that raise theoretical questions that, in turn, lead to
further scientific hypotheses of increased specificity, and so on.
This book is a signal that this process has finally begun. Under the
benevolent nurturing editorship of Phil Richardson and his two co-
editors, an excellent sampler has been provided for those who wish
to engage in the excitement of systematic data gathering that remains the hope of a future for psychoanalysis.

RESEARCH ON
PSYCHOANALYTIC PSYCHOTHERAPY
WITH ADULTS

CHAPTER ONE

The German multi-centre eating disorder study on the influence of psychodynamic psychotherapy on personality

Jörn von Wietersheim, Peter Malewski, Burkard Jäger, Werner Köpp, Ines Gitzinger, Peter Köhler, Ralf Grabhorn, Horst Kächele, & TR-EAT

The eating disorders anorexia nervosa, bulimia nervosa, and the corresponding double diagnoses in the diagnosis schemes DSM–III–R, DSM–IV (Diagnostic and Statistical Manual of Mental Disorders), as well as ICD–10 (International Classification of Diseases) are predominantly defined by symptoms. Additionally, numerous publications (e.g. Feiereis, 1989; Herzog, Stiewe, Sandholz, & Hartmann, 1995; Janssen, Senf, & Meermann, 1997; Senf, 1989), but also clinical experience, have demonstrated that these patients show significant instabilities and disorders with respect to personality traits. Many patients have been reported to suffer from depressive moods, anxieties, low self-esteem, tendencies to social isolation, and, particularly for anorectic patients, compulsive behaviour. As a result, treatments (psychodynamic psychotherapies in particular) seek to tackle these personality characteristics. Treatment of current conflicts as well as strengthening of the resources of individual patients are important goals, in addition to that of reducing the symptoms. Consequently,

This research was funded by the German Ministry of Education and Research (BmBF, FKZ01EN9410).

1

we designed a study that assessed success in terms not only of symptoms, but also of personality and interpersonal relations (Kächele, Kordy, Richard, & Research Group TR-EAT, 2001; Kächele & MZ–ESS, 1999). This report focuses on the measurement of success with respect to personality traits. Personality questionnaires are commonly used to record personality traits and characteristics. High scores on depression, social isolation, enhanced psychopathology, inhibition, powerless self-esteem and reduced life satisfaction have been reported in previous studies on eating disorders, using different questionnaires (Böhle, Wietersheim, Wilke, & Feiereis, 1991; Dancyger, Sunday, Eckert, & Halmi, 1997; Hurt, Brun-Ebérentz, Commerford, Samuel-Lajeuness, & Halmi, 1997; Jäger, Liedtke, Künsebeck, Lempa, Kersting, & Seide, 1996; Schork, Eckert, & Halmi, 1994; Thiel, Züger, Jacoby, & Schüßler, 1999). Anorectic patients (purging type) show higher psychopathology than do restrictive-type patients (Hurt et al., 1997). Dancyger et al. (1997) describe marked changes of the psychopathology during inpatient treatment and fewer changes during the 10-year follow-up period.

This multi-centre eating disorder study (Project TR-EAT) emerged from a combined research effort of various specialized hospitals and university hospitals. The goal of the study was to investigate the courses of anorexia nervosa and bulimia nervosa patients. The focal point of the research was to find out whether or not different periods of inpatient treatment affect the therapy outcome after 2½ years. Further interest was related to the prognosis of these diseases and the possibility of prediction of success at the follow-up evaluation. Numerous symptomatic, but also personality-diagnostic and social variables were recorded by questionnaire and interview at the beginning and the end of an inpatient treatment, as well as at the follow-up examination 2½ years after the beginning of the treatment. In total, 1,247 patients, most of them female, were assessed at the 45 clinics that took part in the study. As a main result, it emerged that 36% of the anorexia patients and likewise 36% of the bulimia patients were largely free of symptoms at the follow-up assessment. The duration (between six weeks and up to more than three months) and intensity (number of psychotherapy sessions) of the inpatient treatment varied greatly. However, these variations did not influence the outcome after 2½ years.

More than 80% of the patients continued psychotherapy after the inpatient treatment, mostly as outpatients, but sometimes as inpatients in another hospital.

However, a distinction must be made between research into personality traits and studies dealing with personality disorders of patients with eating disorders. Personality disorders are well-defined (e.g. according to DSM–IV or ICD–10) diagnoses, which can be drawn in addition to an existing eating disorder and describe a serious psychopathology. Accordingly, the co-morbidity of anorexia and personality disorders has been estimated to be up to approximately 50% (Rosenvinge & Mouland, 1990). Estimates of bulimic patients with additional personality disorders are in the range of 20% (Herzog et al., 1995). For the assessment of treatment success the use of a personality disorder co-morbidity is likely to be less sensitive than is the standardized assessment of personality traits.

Method

This work is a partial evaluation carried out in the context of the multi-centre eating disorder study (Kächele & MZ–ESS, 1999, 2000). Only the methodological aspects relevant to this evaluation are considered here.

The instruments used for personality data collection were the *Freiburger Persönlichkeitsinventar* [Freiburg Personality Inventory] [FPI–R] (Fahrenberg, Hampel, & Selg, 1989) and the *Narzissmusinventar* [*Narcissism inventory*] (Deneke & Hilgenstock, 1989). The FPI–R was set as the German standard assessment instrument for personality data. Since problems of the narcissistic regulatory system are commonly associated with eating disorder patients, the *narcissism inventory* was also used. For reasons of economy, however, a third of the scales have been discarded, as no deviation from a "healthy" control group could be found in previous studies. The internal consistency (Cronbach's Alpha) of the narcissism inventory scales lies between 0.71 and 0.94. Overlap with the FPI–R is only marginal.

Data on personality were recorded at the beginning and the end of an inpatient treatment, which lasted, on average, approximately three months, as well as at the time of the follow-up evaluation 2½ years after admission into the inpatient treatment.

Four levels of symptomatic success were defined according to the DSM–III–R diagnostic criteria. The components used in each case were the main symptom: for anorexia nervosa, being under-weight (15% below the expected weight), for bulimia, binging (at least twice a week), as well as other symptoms such as body image distortion, fear of fatness, and weight-reduction strategies. The assessment of success was scaled as follows: 0 = "all relevant symptoms are pathological"; 1 = "one symptom in the healthy range"; 2 = "the main symptom (weight or binges, respectively) and one additional symptom in the healthy range"; 3 = "all symp-toms in the healthy range".

It is very problematic and dubious to define a single criterion for success in the personality field. Based on experience with these instruments, a criterion has been developed, which contained four scales that were considered necessary; these were derived from the FPI–R scales for "life satisfaction" and "self-consciousness" and from the narcissism inventory for "powerless self" and "negative body-self". These scales were selected as they reflect important aspects of specific problems of patients with eating disorders on the one hand, and, on the other hand, cover different content areas. A further consideration regarding the definition of success was that the main goal of therapy should be to improve pathological (deviating from the normal range) values in the relevant scales, and to reach norm-values if possible. Hence, if a value falls outside the normal range before treatment but inside after it, then this should be considered a success (corresponding to one point in the success criterion). If a value improves clinically significantly, but still lies outside the normal range (e.g. improvement of stanine values from 1 to 3), this should be considered a partial success (half a point). Here, a definition of a clinically significant change, which is related to the reliability of an instrument (questionnaire), has been used (Jacobson & Truax, 1991). Consequently, a criterion to measure success has been developed, which considered both absolute changes (outside before treatment and inside after it) and relative changes (strongly pathological before treatment, clinically signifi-cantly less pathological after). If a value has been in the normal range right from the start, then the therapy was judged successful concerning the respective scale. (This could lead to an over-estimation of the effectiveness of therapy, but this rarely occurred.) The success points were added up, and a metric standard for success was constructed with them. The value 6 corresponds to maximum success, reflecting the maximum change, the value 0 denotes no change in personality values, and negative values (to a maximum of –2) indicate deterioration.

All patients were admitted to one of 45 psychodynamically orientated psychotherapeutic hospitals in Germany between September 1993 and October 1995. The 2½-year follow-up assessment was conducted by the end of 1998. Inclusion criteria were DSM–III–R diagnosis for anorexia nervosa and bulimia nervosa and double diagnosis (both anorexia and bulimia criteria fulfilled), as well as an age of ≥18 years. Originally 1,247 mostly female patients participated in this study; however, owing to data inconsistencies, the sample size decreased to 1,171 participants.

The following description of the samples is for the 732 patients who participated in the follow-up: 712 patients were female, 20 were male; 405 were bulimic, 229 anorectic, and 98 cases were double diagnoses. The average age of anorectic patients was 24.9 ($SD = 6.0$) years, that of bulimic patients 25.9 ($SD = 6.3$) years, and that of patients with a double diagnosis 25.4 ($SD = 5.7$). years The average duration of illness for anorectic patients was 5.8 years ($SD = 5.4$), for bulimic patients 8.2 years ($SD = 6.2$), and for patients with double diagnosis 6.7 years ($SD = 5.5$). The average duration of inpatient treatment was 12.2 weeks ($SD = 7.7$).

As yet, there are no normative data available for the narcissism inventory. Thus, data from a control group, consisting of 120 female medical students, have been used (data courtesy of K. Engel, Dortmund).

Results

Freiburger personality inventory

Table 1.1 depicts the FPI–R–stanine values for the anorexia and bulimia group. Many scales show changes in the means that are

Table 1.1. FPI scales (Stanine)ᵃ for "admission", "release", and "follow-up"

FPI	Anorexiaᵇ			Bulimiaᶜ		
	Admission	Discharge	Follow-up	Admission	Discharge	Follow-up
Life satisfaction	2.7 ±1.4	3.1 ±1.6	3.5 ±1.8	2.7 ±1.2	3.1 ±1.4	3.6 ±1.8
Social orientation	5.9 ±1.8	5.5 ±1.7	5.1 ±1.8	5.6 ±1.8	5.1 ±1.9	5.0 ±1.8
Efficiency orientation	4.8 ±1.9	5.2 ±1.9	5.1 ±1.9	4.5 ±1.9	4.9 ±1.9	4.8 ±2.0
Inhibition	6.8 ±1.9	6.4 ±1.8	6.1 ±2	6.4 ±2	6.0 ±2.0	5.9 ±2.1
Arousal	6.4 ±1.7	6.3 ±1.8	6.2 ±1.8	6.4 ±1.8	6.3 ±1.8	6.2 ±1.9
Aggressiveness	4.6 ±1.9	4.8 ±1.9	4.9 ±1.7	5.2 ±1.9	5.4 ±2.0	5.4 ±1.7
Strain	6.1 ±1.5	5.8 ±1.6	5.7 ±1.7	6.1 ±1.6	5.8 ±1.7	5.7 ±1.8
Physical complaints	6.8 ±1.9	6.1 ±2	6.2 ±2.1	6.7 ±1.7	6.1 ±1.8	5.7 ±2.0
Health concerns	4.3 ±2.1	4.3 ±2.1	4.0 ±2.1	3.7 ±1.8	3.9 ±2.0	4.0 ±2.0
Openness	5.3 ±1.8	5.4 ±1.8	5.3 ±1.8	6.0 ±1.8	6.0 ±1.9	6.0 ±1.7
Extraversion	3.4 ±1.9	4.0 ±1.9	3.9 ±1.9	4.1 ±2.1	4.6 ±2.1	4.4 ±2.0
Emotionality	7.1 ±1.6	6.8 ±1.9	6.6 ±2.0	7.3 ±1.4	6.9 ±1.7	6.6 ±2.0

ᵃMeans ± standard deviations; ᵇanorexia: N = 229; ᶜbulimia: N = 405.

rather small numerically—and probably also clinically. Particularly obvious are very low life satisfaction, high inhibition, high arousal, and high emotionality (neuroticism). Changes of the means in the desired direction became apparent in the previously defined scales for the measurement of success. Also, many of the patients show clinically deviating personality characteristics (stanine values < 4 and > 6, respectively). Changes take place in the period between admission and discharge as well as between discharge and the date of follow-up evaluation. Patients with a double diagnosis—which, owing to lack of space, are not included in Table 1.1—displayed particularly low values for "life satisfaction", but also particularly high values for "strain" and "emotionality". These patients seem to have a higher psychopathology.

Narcissism inventory

Table 1.2 shows the scales of the narcissism inventory. Here, too, changes in the mean values became apparent, even more than was the case with FPI–R. Significant changes can be seen between admission and discharge on the scales for "negative body-self", "powerless self", "de-realization/depersonalization", and "diminished self-image". These effects are apparent in all three diagnostic groups. Accordingly, after inpatient treatment the patients learn to accept their bodies slightly better, and they feel less powerless and inferior. Overall, greater changes seem to take place between inpatient admission and discharge than between discharge and the follow-up assessment, although most patients experienced outpatient psychotherapy after inpatient treatment. Clearly, distinct effects of intense inpatient psychotherapy can be seen from these questionnaires.

Table 1.2. Scales of the narcissism inventory[a] for "admission", "release", and "follow-up"

Narcissism inventory	Anorexia[b]			Bulimia[c]		
	Admission	Discharge	Follow-up	Admission	Discharge	Follow-up
Powerless self	32.3 ±9.7	27.2 ±10.1	27.1 ±11.2	33.1 ±9.5	27.3 ±10.0	26.1 ±10.9
Loss of affect impulse control	30.7 ±8.5	28.6 ±8.9	27.9 ±9.1	33.3 ±8.8	30.2 ±8.6	29.2 ±9.1
Derealization/ de-personalization	29.9 ±10.7	25.3 ±10.6	24.7 ±11.7	29.8 ±10.5	25.0 ±10.3	24.0 ±11.1
Basic hope potential	30.2 ±9.3	32.1 ±9.6	32.3 ±9.5	28.9 ±9.4	32.0 ±9.6	33.8 ±9.7
Diminished self-image	35.1 ±8.7	31.9 ±9.0	32.3 ±9.3	34.9 ±8.8	31.2 ±8.9	30.3 ±9.3
Negative body-self	30.0 ±11.1	24.5 ±10.9	25.2 ±12.5	31.2 ±11.4	24.7 ±11.4	24.0 ±12.2
Social isolation	30.8 ±8.6	28.5 ±8.6	28.3 ±8.7	29.4 ±8.6	27.5 ±8.2	27.1 ±9.0
Greatness self	24.3 ±7.0	26.1 ±6.9	26.7 ±6.8	26.4 ±7.4	28.2 ±7	28.8 ±7.2
Narcissistic rage	26.8 ±8.1	26.6 ±7.7	26.4 ±7.6	28.1 ±8.1	27.8 ±7.6	27.3 ±7.8
Object devaluation	26.9 ±7.1	25.4 ±7.3	26.7 ±7.7	28.7 ±7.2	26.7 ±7.5	27.0 ±7.6
Symbiontic self-protection	38.7 ±5.7	36 ±6.3	37.4 ±6.4	37.6 ±6.5	35.4 ±6.6	36.7 ±6.5
Hypochondriac anxiety bonds	26.1 ±9.4	23 ±9.3	22.7 ±9.6	25.7 ±9.0	22.5 ±8.5	23.1 ±9.1
Narcissistic illness gain	24.6 ±9.3	22.6 ±9.3	21.4 ±10.3	21.4 ±8.7	19.0 ±8.1	19.4 ±8.9

[a]Means ± standard deviations; [b]anorexia: N = 229; [c]bulimia: N = 405.

A comparison between the groups of patients with eating disorders and the control group (120 female medical students) revealed significant deviations on many scales. Particularly significant differences emerged on the "powerless self", "de-realization", "diminished self-image", "negative body-image", and "social isolation" scales. Known clinical signs and symptoms are hence well reflected in the questionnaire data for these patients.

Calculation and distribution of the success criterion

Figure 1.1 shows the number of patients who deviated from the normal range on the four target criteria scales at the point of admission and at the follow-up assessment. The largest group deviated from the normal range on all four target scales. In contrast, 4% of patients fell within the normal range on these scales (despite an apparent eating disorder). Some change is visible from the time of admission to follow-up assessment. A few patients who had previously been outside the defined normal range now fell within it; in all, only about 20% of patients experienced this degree of change, with the majority remaining within the pathological range on the scales.

The success criterion used in this study was developed on the basis of the clinically significant change criterion of Jacobson and Truax (1991). It is composed of absolute values (whether or not a patient is within the normal range of a respective scale) and the values for changes (whether or not a patient has changed significantly clinically since admission). Figure 1.2 shows the distribution of the success criterion for the groups of anorexia and bulimia nervosa patients. A relatively large group (13%) of patients shows no evidence of change, and a further 13% of the patients show evidence of deterioration during the course of treatment. For the majority of the patients, however, there is an indication of improvement, which show a relatively wide deviation. Approximately a third of the patients show distinct improvement (value of success ³ 3). Comparing the three diagnosis groups, it becomes apparent that anorexia and bulimia patients show similar success ratios, whereas patients with double diagnosis show significantly less evidence of success.

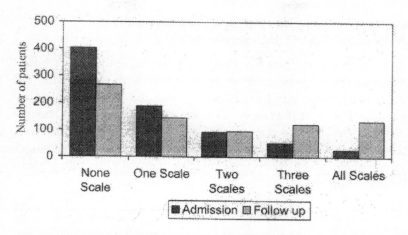

Figure 1.1. Number of patients and personality scales outside the norm: FPI scales for "life satisfaction" and "arousal" as well as, from the narcissism inventory, those for "powerless self" and "negative body-self".

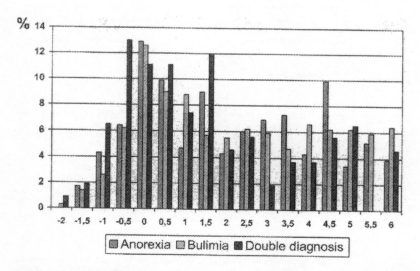

Figure 1.2. Distribution of percentages for the success criterion "personality" for each diagnosis group. The criterion is the sum of the scales that were within the norm (coded [0,1]) at follow-up and the number of scales that showed clinically significant changes since admission (coded [0,½]).

Relations between the criteria for improvement on personality and symptom measures

These relations are shown in Figure 1.3 (the symptomatic criterion in four levels, the personality criterion scaled to the interval). Good agreement can be seen from these illustrations. They are however not really linear, as the respective correlations (Spearman's rho) for anorexia was 0.52, for bulimia 0.35 and for double diagnoses 0.27. According to that, change in personality corresponds with changes in symptoms. The direction of causality, if any, in this relationship remains unclear.

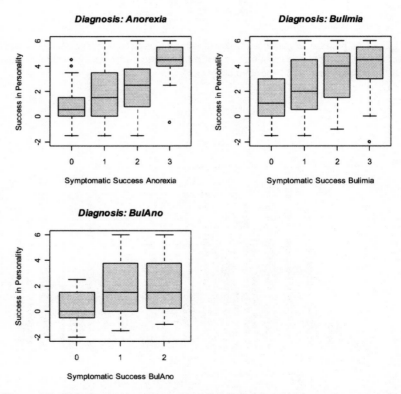

Figure 1.3. Relation between symptomatic success and success in personality scales. Symptomatic success: 0 = all relevant symptoms outside the norm; 1 = 1 symptom within the norm; 2 = main symptom—weight or binges—and another symptom within the norm; 3 = all relevant symptoms within the norm. No patient in the group with double diagnosis (BulAno) reached a value of 3 for symptomatic success.

Prediction

To what extent is prediction of a positive outcome possible on the personality measures? For this, two models were modified and successively tested. The first model tested the association of relevant patient traits with the degree of patient improvement. The second model tested whether or not the therapy parameters (duration of inpatient treatment, number of therapy sessions) influenced the degree of improvement. To compensate for model violations, the response variable has been transformed according to the BoxCox transformation (lambda = .24).

Two combined measures, which characterized the symptomatic state at admission, have been applied as potential predictors. Further predictors include the extent of pre-treatment, the duration of illness, the patient's weight (body-mass index: BMI), their desired weight, the overall SCL–90 (Symptom Checklist) value, as well as the sum of the three EDI scales: drive for thinness, bulimia, body dissatisfaction. The calculated first model, however, only clarifies 5% of the variance (adjusted). For the second model, the amount of therapy was considered, in terms of the total number (duration of inpatient treatment) of days and the weekly "dose" in hours. Likewise within this expanded model, only 5% of the variance could be accounted for. Accordingly, prediction before treatment as to later therapeutic success in the personality domain was not possible, at least with the variables employed in the present study.

Discussion

Both the Freiburger Personality Inventory and the Narcissism Inventory reflect clinically known psychopathological signs and symptoms of patients with eating disorders. It has to be emphasized, however, that regardless of their ascertained diagnoses of eating disorder, not all patients deviated from the normal range in the questionnaire values. There was a small number of eating disorder patients with normal questionnaire values. It is possible that these patients were dissimulating; but it is also conceivable that they developed anorectic or bulimic reactions to an acute crisis, with the personality, in fact, remaining relatively unaffected.

The score distributions are relatively broad—that is, the patients are very different. Changes that are reflected in the questionnaire values occurred during inpatient treatment, but also during subsequent outpatient treatment.

Nevertheless, most patients did not return to normal during the observation period. They felt slightly better, but the majority did not reach the values of a norm-group (FPI–R) or a healthy control group in the narcissism inventory, respectively. This can be seen to be paralleled by the successful outcomes where symptoms were concerned: most patients showed marked eating disorder symptoms after 2½ years of observation, and only about 36% were considered clinically healthy (Kächele & MZ–ESS, 2000).

These slow and limited changes in the questionnaire values of the FPI and narcissism inventory closely match theoretical considerations as to personality and eating disorders. Personality is considered an enduring construct, which evolves and changes only very slowly. In addition, clinical experience from work with patients with eating disorders corresponds to these results: changes happen only gradually. It is clear that changes on the narcissism inventory appear more frequently during the three months (on average) of inpatient treatment; fewer changes occur in the follow-up period, when most patients receive outpatient therapy. These findings support and justify such intensive psychotherapeutic procedures as inpatient treatment. Dancyger et al. (1997) reported very similar results in a study of anorexic patients by means of the MMPI (Minnesota Multiphasic Inventory) at hospital admission, discharge, and follow-up evaluation.

Direct comparisons between change (successful outcomes) in the fields of personality and symptoms show moderate agreement. Symptomatic improvement went along with improvements in the domain of personality; the correlation coefficients (Spearman's Rho), however, were only of moderate strength. The question of whether changes in the fields of personality and apparent symptoms coincide or take place in succession, and whether change in one field—e.g. personality—is a requirement for change in another—e.g. symptoms—remains unclear and will be the subject of future investigation.

Successful prediction of improvement in the personality domain could not be achieved. Change in personality could also not be explained by patient variables such as degree of apparent symptoms, duration of illness, number of previous treatments, and so on, or by therapy variables, such as duration and intensity of inpatient therapy. The variance accounted for in each case was only around 5%. These results correspond to those reported by Kächele et al. (2001) related to success regarding apparent symptoms; these also indicated no safe method for prediction.

Consequently, parameters affecting the changes shown by inpatients with eating disorders remain unclear. This problem should be the subject of future investigation, which should include a discussion on the relatively short duration of follow-up. It is conceivable that after 2½ years many patients are still in the process of symptomatic and personality-related development and that recognizable effects only become apparent at a later stage of the course of their illness.

CHAPTER TWO

Differential treatment outcome of inpatient psychodynamic group work

Bernhard Strauss & Silke Schmidt

Background: The German Working Group on Inpatient Group Psychotherapy

For historical reasons psychotherapy in Germany has a very specific tradition (cf. Strauss & Kächele, 1998). Part of this tradition is the great importance placed on inpatient psychotherapy. Genuine psychotherapeutic hospitals had already been founded in Germany even before the Second World War (such as by Georg Simmel in Berlin and by Georg Groddeck in Baden-Baden), and after the War numerous psychotherapeutic hospitals were added to these, as well as several hospitals for psychotherapeutic and psychosomatic rehabilitation. This has contributed to the fact that Germany has still well over 10,000 hospital beds for psychotherapy alone, in addition to those within psychiatry. Accordingly, inpatient psychotherapy has become a very important part of the psychotherapy delivery system in this country.

Compared to publications dealing with the development and differentiation of treatment concepts within the inpatient field, empirical studies remained rare until the 1980s (Strauss, 1992).

15

With the foundation, in 1988, of the Mainz Workshop on Research in Inpatient Psychotherapy (by M. Bassler and S. O. Hoffmann), empirical research received a new impetus, resulting in several initiatives to study the process and outcome of inpatient treatments. Related to the Mainz workshop, several working groups were established. These working groups tried to focus on specific research questions in the field and to organize cooperation between university hospitals and other psychotherapeutic hospitals. The German Working Group on Inpatient Group Psychotherapy was founded in 1990 by B. Strauss and J. Eckert (Hamburg University). The major goal of the research network was to consider the importance of group work within the inpatient setting. In general, there is a considerable lack of studies focusing on the process and outcome of psychodynamic group treatments (Fonagy et al., 1999) in comparison to individual therapy.

At present, the research group consists of colleagues from ten university hospitals or institutions (Hamburg, Leipzig, Bielefeld, Innsbruck, Kiel, Mainz, Jena, Göttingen, Hannover, Düsseldorf) and eight general psychotherapeutic or rehabilitation hospitals (Hamburg, Berlin, Grönenbach, Bad Honnef, Geldern, Bad Kreuznach, Frankfurt/Oder, Bad Segeberg). The programme of the group is to organize multi-site studies focusing on very specific questions in the field of inpatient group psychotherapy. In general, the intention is to run these studies in naturalistic settings, with a design that should be easy to integrate into the clinical routine, making the raising of specific funds unnecessary.

Since its foundation, the working group has completed a variety of studies on the assignment of patients to different subsettings (Eckert et al., 1997), quality assurance in inpatient groups (Strauss, Kriebel, & Mattke, 1998), or the predictive value of attachment styles for the outcome of inpatient groups (e.g. Strauss, Lobo-Drost, & Pilkonis, 1999). One major focus of the work during the last ten years concerns the question as to whether the degree and kind of interpersonal problems reported by patients at admission is of any value in differentially predicting the outcome of inpatient psychodynamic group treatment; this research is summarized in this chapter.

The general research question:
do interpersonal problems predict treatment outcome?

Research on inpatient psychodynamic group work has focused on various questions during the last years (Strauss, 1992)—namely, the investigation of its global effectiveness (e.g. Strauss & Burgmeier-Lohse, 1994), the subjective importance of single components of the inpatient programme for the patients (e.g. von Rad, Senf, & Bräutigam, 1998), the study of therapeutic factors (e.g. Strauss & Burgmeier-Lohse, 1995), and process research (e.g. Tschuschke, 1993). The working group has primarily focused on the question of how the patients' experience of their interpersonal problems—as assessed by the Inventory of Interpersonal Problems (IIP) (Horowitz, Strauss, & Kordy, 1994)—can predict the outcome of group treatment. This question is based upon the observation that interpersonal relationships, their structure, dynamics, and adaptability, play an important role in the course and outcome of psychodynamic psychotherapy. The interpersonal model, which has its origins in the psychoanalytic literature (e.g. Horney, 1945), has been shown to be relevant for describing human behaviour in psychotherapy.

In our studies it was assumed that the degree and the quality of interpersonal problems as reported by patients undergoing inpatient group treatment should be a differential indicator of treatment outcome. This assumption was based on studies from other fields of psychotherapy showing that interpersonal problems might be significant factors enabling the differentiation of patients with varying degrees of treatment success (e.g. Horowitz, Rosenberg, & Bartholomew, 1993; Mohr et al., 1990). Before we undertook our research, no data were available regarding this question in the inpatient setting. Specifically, we expected that patients who were aware of their interpersonal difficulties should be more responsive to psychodynamic treatment approaches, whereas those who did not experience interpersonal complaints might be better assigned to other treatment approaches.

Three studies have now been conducted within the working group, and these are summarized here. Data related to the most recent study (Study 3) have not yet been published; the finding of the other two studies have also been reported elsewhere (Davies-Osterkamp, Strauss, & Schmitz, 1996; Strauss, Eckert, & Ott, 1993).

Central research method: The Inventory of Interpersonal Problems

Based upon the observation that the most frequent complaint of patients upon entering psychotherapy is that they find it difficult to get on with other people, Horowitz and co-workers (Horowitz, Rosenberg, Baer, Ureno, & Villasenor, 1988) compiled the IIP, which has now become a standard instrument in psychotherapy research (Strupp, Horowitz, & Lambert, 1997). The questionnaire originally covered 127 items describing common interpersonal difficulties. Whereas some of these items begin with the statement "It is hard for me . . ." (to do something, such as to say "no" to other people), other items indicate that the person does certain things too much (e.g. "I fight with other people too much"). Horowitz, Rosenberg, Baer, et al. (1988) demonstrated that—according to the assumptions of the interpersonal model—the items of the IIP could be arranged along the two orthogonal axes "affection" (friendliness vs. hostility) and "control" (dominance vs. submission). Alden, Wiggins, and Pincus (1990) showed that the items fit into a circumplex structure (Figure 2.1) and constructed eight subscales of eight items each (i.e. a total of 64), each covering an eighth, or an octant, of the two-dimensional model.

Study 1

The first study testing the major hypothesis was carried out with the participation of eight hospitals, all providing similar forms of psychodynamically oriented group treatment; 470 patients from these hospitals were included in this study, and the results were analysed individually for each institution (for a comprehensive description of the detailed results, see the special issue of the journal *Gruppenpsychotherapie und Gruppendynamik* [Group psychotherapy and Group dynamics], Strauss, Eckert, & Ott, 1993).

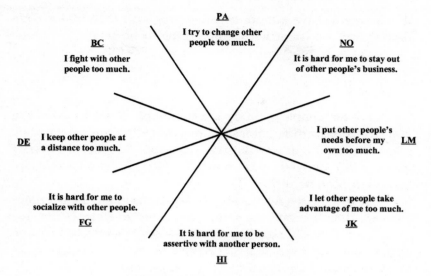

PA
I try to change other
people too much.

BC
I fight with other
people too much.

NO
It is hard for me to stay out
of other people's business.

DE   I keep other people at
a distance too much.

I put other people's
needs before my   LM
own too much.

It is hard for me to
socialize with other people.
FG

I let other people take
advantage of me too much.
JK

It is hard for me to be
assertive with another person.
HI

Figure 2.1. Interpersonal circumplex

Of the 470 patients participating in this study, 66% were female. The mean age of the patients was 31, with an age range between 17 and 59 years ($SD = 11.8$) Individual hospitals contributed to the study with patient numbers varying between 24 and 110. Although the concepts of the group treatment were similar, the general treatment programmes differed with respect to the length of the inpatient therapy, with the shortest programme lasting five–six weeks and the longest six–seven months. Owing to the fact that the individual hospitals used their own criteria for the assessment of treatment outcome, it was difficult to integrate the individual findings (Strauss, Eckert, & Hess, 1993). Nevertheless, some general trends could be discerned.

Patients suffering mainly from interpersonal distress—as compared to symptomatic distress, as measured with the SCL–90–R—gained more benefit from the inpatient group treatment in a setting with a shorter treatment length (Muhs, 1993), whereas patients predominantly suffering from symptomatic distress had a better outcome in long-term group treatment (Strauss & Burgmeier-Lohse, 1993).

As far as specific interpersonal problems were concerned, there was a tendency for patients suffering from problems with hostile dominance to have a more negative prognosis than others. This finding was consistent across three of the six hospitals.

Study 2

Out of the sample of Study 1, a subsample was selected of 194 patients from six different institutions providing comparable data sets with respect to one outcome measure: the Global Severity Index (GSI) derived from the SCL–90–R (Davies-Osterkamp, Strauss, & Schmitz, 1996).

To determine the relationship between the interpersonal problems at admission and the symptom-related treatment outcome, criteria for clinically significant changes were determined [*critical change value*, kb = x_{norm} + $2s_{norm}$; *reliable change*, RC = (x_{post} – x_{pre})/ s_{diff}; i.e. standard error of difference: see Jacobson & Truax, 1991].

Overall, the effect size for the SCL–90–R changes was .57; for changes in interpersonal problems (total IIP score), it was .30. Using the criteria for clinically relevant improvement, four groups of patients could be distinguished:

- patients whose condition deteriorated (9.3%)
- patients with no perceptible changes (26.8%)
- patients whose symptoms improved (29.4%)
- patients whose discharge values in the SCL–90–R fell into a normal range (20.2%)

An additional subgroup of 14.4% of patients showed normal SCL–90–R scores at admission as well as at discharge ("healthy" subgroup).

In this study, the main goals were to discover whether patients who were more aware of their interpersonal problems before treatment began would have a better prognosis in inpatient group psychotherapy in terms of symptomatic change. It turned out that particularly those patients who were rated as "cured" or "improved" by the end of therapy on the basis of their SCL–90–R measures had reported the most interpersonal problems before their treatment had begun [$F(1, 189) = 6.7, p < .05$] (Figure 2.2).

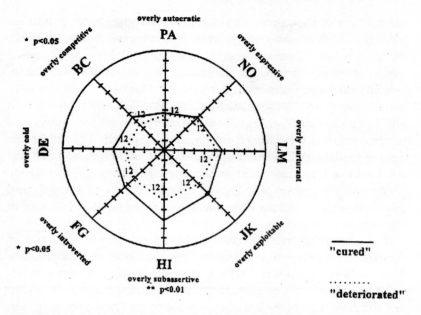

Figure 2.2. Interpersonal profile at admission of patients who were cured versus those whose condition deteriorated (Davies-Osterkamp, Strauss, & Schmitz, 1996)

Study 3

The overall objective of the Multicentre Study 3 was not only to replicate findings of the preceding studies on a larger scale, but also to further evaluate the differential and prognostic validity of various facets of interpersonal problems. The aim was to examine the prediction of outcome by interpersonal problems, thus addressing the "interpersonalness" of the treatment outcome. More specific research questions were to explore whether using ipsatized or unipsatized scores of the IIP would have any impact on this prediction (see below) and whether the interpersonal profile is related to changes in interpersonal problems and to personality-related outcome.

Data for this study were collected within six different hospitals with different treatment settings (Kiel, Bad Honnef, Groenenbach, Goettingen, Geldern, Haldensleben). Again, the common element of the settings was the use of psychodynamic group work as a central part of each programme. Measures common to all settings were the IIP (German version: Horowitz, Strauss, & Kordy, 1994), the SCL–90–R (German version: Franke, 1992), and the Giessen Test (Beckmann, Brähler, & Richter, 1990), which is a psychoanalytically oriented personality inventory that is very commonly used in Germany. These measures were assessed at least twice—on admission and at discharge. In three of the six centres individual treatment goals were also formulated and recorded at the beginning of treatment. The extent (percentage) to which these goals had been attained was assessed at the end of treatment by both the patient and the therapist. Finally, global ratings of somatic and psychological treatment outcome were given by the therapist at discharge.

For a better appreciation of the interpretation of the results, it is necessary to comment on some specific aspects of the instruments: The Giessen Personality Test has its roots in the German psychoanalytic and social psychology tradition. However, it is intended not so much to capture individual traits but, rather, to conceptualize aspects of personality as they manifest themselves in dyadic relationships or in group processes. The 40 items, using bipolar 7-point scales, include questions on emotional states, questions on ego qualities (such as introspection, imagination, and permeability), questions on interpersonal states (such as self-disclosure), and questions on social reactions and/or responses by others. A factor analysis of the items yielded six scales.

The first scale, called "social response", gauges the positive or negative feedback a person receives from the environment on the basis of his/her personality. The second scale, "dominance", assesses whether a person is more flexible, accommodating, and obsequious, or more domineering in social relationships. The "self-control" scale is less conceptualized from an interpersonal stance and addresses whether a person is more self-controlled, and even obsessive-compulsive, or more disorganized in his or her personal affairs. The fourth scale, "underlying mood", represents a (hypo)-manic-depressive dimension. The "permeability" scale assesses whether a person is more open, self-disclosing, and permeable, or more retentive and reserved. The sixth scale, "social potency", describes whether somebody is able to achieve his or her social goals in a maximally adaptive way.

The original factor analysis was based upon a sample of psychotherapy patients from the University Hospital Giessen. The five-factor solution accounted for 58% of the variance. Beckmann, Brähler, and Richter (1990) report several replications of the factorial structure in different clinical and non-clinical samples.

The Giessen Test is not considered to be a genuine tool of psychotherapeutic outcome measurement. However, it has proved to be sensitive to change in specific contexts—that is, in identifying psychotherapeutic treatment outcome (Stuhr, 1997), or changes in the self-concepts of the German population during societal changes (Brähler & Richter, 2000). Because it was developed from a psychoanalytic and social psychology tradition, it has considerable face validity as a clinically relevant outcome measure for inpatients.

With regard to the IIP, it is important to note that two different interpretations of the circumplex of interpersonal problems exist. These different lines of interpretation have emerged since interpersonal problems are considered to be the counterparts of interpersonal traits. In the tradition of circumplex models, these traits represent the vectors in a two-dimensional circular space formed by the coordinates of affiliation (LOVE) and dominance (DOM). The eight scales (Figure 2.1) usually identify particular patterns of interpersonal tendencies. Wiggins, Phillips, and Trapnell (1989) as well as Gurtman (1991) have proposed that subjects should be classified according to the typological sector of the interpersonal circle in which they fall. This is defined by the average directional tendency of their interpersonal behaviour with reference to the coordinates of love and dominance. Ambiguous definitions of the interpersonal tendency have emerged when applying the interpersonal problems counterpart to this conceptual framework.

First, the typological sector of a person may be interpreted according to the content of the scale—that is, these categories represent the interpersonal field that distresses the person to the highest extent. In this vein, one can imagine that a patient who suffers from being too obedient and too submissive in interpersonal relationships may also overtly complain about interpersonal disturbances related to assertiveness and dominance and not only to submissiveness.

The second interpretation is much more common and defines the category as an individual's interpersonal focus or tendency—

that is, an area that is the focus of the person's inner attention and that leads to the most characteristic and precarious interpersonal conflicts. In line with this interpretation, Alden, Wiggins, and Pincus (1990) were able to show high convergent validity between interpersonal traits, as measured with the Revised Interpersonal Adjective Scales, and interpersonal problems. This finding indicates that it is, rather, the content of the scales or interpersonal areas that is evoked by the IIP items. A way to deal with these ambiguities is to use *unipsatized scores* when the literal meaning of the scales is more important and to use *ipsatized scores* when the interpersonal tendency or focus has a higher validity. Ipsatizing is accomplished by subtracting an individual's mean from each IIP scale mean. Using the IIP in this large sample, we wished to elucidate these concurrent notions of the interpersonal tendency in a clinical population.

Following a replication of the findings from Study 2, the analytic strategy behind this work was primarily to run multiple regression analyses to predict treatment outcome and, secondly, to evaluate the impact of the interpersonal profile on the eight octants, respectively, on changes in interpersonal and personality-related measures. These research questions are part of a larger project, which also addresses the relationship between interpersonal problems and conventions of clinical and statistical significance on the one hand and interpersonal problems and diagnostic categories, especially personality disorders, on the other. Thus, we present selected results related to the clinical validity of the IIP.

Sample characteristics

Complete data for the IIP and SCL–90–R were obtained from about 740 patients at both points of measurement. Approximately 600 patients completed the Giessen Test twice. However, the goal attainment and global outcome ratings were only assessed in three hospitals. 350 global outcome ratings were collected in these centres; 260 patients and 120 therapists assessed the extent to which the initial treatment goals had been reached.

Of the subsample of patients who completed the questionnaires at admission and at discharge, 67% were female and 33% were male. The mean age of these patients was 38 (±9.5; range: 17 to 63). The global diagnoses represented in this sample were personality disorders (22%), eating disorders (21%), anxiety, dissociative and somatoform disorders (22%), affective disorders (19%), substance abuse (5%) and psychoses (0.5%).

Replications of findings on the relationship between clinically significant change and interpersonal problems

Applying the conventions of clinical and statistical significance, 25% of the sample fell into the "healthy" or "normal range" category, 28% improved in clinically and statistically significant terms ("cured") and 15% remained unchanged. 14% of all patients were assigned to the category "deteriorated" (statistically and/or clinically significant). These proportions are very similar to those identified in the second study.

Again, those patients who deteriorated showed the *lowest level of interpersonal problems* and the *least differentiated interpersonal profile*. It should be noted, however, that some contrasting findings related to this group were obtained from the global outcome ratings and goal attainment scaling of the therapists. Contrary to expectations, the outcome ratings of the therapists were highest for patients who deteriorated on the SCL–90–R! These latter patients were also the only group that had higher scores on all interpersonal problem scales *at discharge* regardless of the area to which they were related, as shown in Figure 2.3.

The interpersonal profile of the IIP pre- and post-treatment scores shown in Figure 2.3 contrasts sharply with the profile of patients who did improve (Figure 2.4): these patients, who improved according to statistical and clinical criteria, complained less about interpersonal problems, especially about those located in the lower octants (too submissive), while problems with being overly autocratic were reported more often.

The fact that patients who deteriorated in clinically and statistically significant terms reported only few interpersonal problems on admission yet more problems at discharge could have led their therapists to globally rate a positive treatment outcome. A more detailed discussion of these findings will be provided by Strauss,

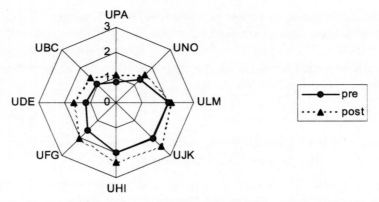

Figure 2.3. Interpersonal problems on admission and at discharge in patients who deteriorated statistically and clinically.

Schmidt, and the working group on inpatient group therapy (in preparation).

Prediction of treatment outcome on the basis of the quality of interpersonal problems

To test whether the quality of interpersonal problems (i.e. the pattern of scores on the eight subscales) can predict outcome, multiple regression analyses were performed in two steps: we first

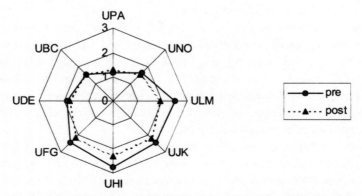

Figure 2.4. Interpersonal problems on admission and at discharge in patients who improved statistically and clinically.

included the unipsatized scores and then, in a second step, the ipsatized scores as predictors into the equation. In both equations the mean score of the IIP was included as well as a predictor variable in order to explore whether the total quantity of interpersonal problems or specific aspects have a higher prognostic impact. Criterion variables were (1) the difference score on the GSI; (2) the difference scores on the scales of the Giessen Test; and (3) the global outcome ratings, as well as the goal-attainment scales.

Because of the nature of the circumplex, a high degree of multicollinearity has to be taken into account when interpreting findings. The correlations between the IIP total score and the single scales were highest in HI (too unassertive), FG (too socially avoidant), and JK (too exploitable). Thus, the predictive power of one of these scales might easily be suppressed by the others.

Predictions of goal attainment and global outcome ratings

In predicting the goal attainment ratings and the global outcome for both patient and therapist, interpersonal problems had a significant effect only on the therapists' global ratings of the psychological outcome ($R^2 = .7, p < .001$). In this regression, nonassertiveness at admission had a significant impact on a better global psychological treatment outcome as rated by the therapist. This is consistent with the findings of Horowitz, Rosenberg, and Bartholomew (1993). They concluded that problems with friendly submissiveness seem to be more easily treated in brief dynamic psychotherapy than are problems concerning hostile dominance.

Prediction of improvement in the Global Severity Index

In predicting the change in the GSI, both the regression equation including ipsatized scores and that including unipsatized scores were found to be significant. Interpersonal problems explained approximately 12% of the variance of change on the GSI. In both equations, only the IIP total score, but none of the single scales, were found to have a significant effect on change in the GSI scores ($F = 19.60, p < .001$).

Prediction of change on the scales
of the personality inventory (Giessen Test)

In predicting change on the scales of the Giessen Test, the single scales showed a greater predictive potential than did the total IIP scores (Table 2.1).

In general, all equations predicting change in the scales of the Giessen Test, based on interpersonal problems, were significant, with the exception of change on the "self-control" scale. Another general finding was that a decrease in the depression scale was predicted by the IIP total score, but neither of the single subscales proved to be significant. However, the single IIP scales had a significant impact on changes in the four Giessen Test subscales, which more strongly reflect relational dimensions.

The prognostic effects of the IIP scales were overall highly significant, irrespective of the fact that ipsatized or unipsatized scores were used as predictors. Because of the high multicollinearity of the IIP scales, it is difficult to compare the effect of using ipsatized and unipsatized scores in the regression equations.

The impact of the interpersonal focus
on changes in the Giessen Test

In addition to the regression analysis, a finer analysis of the validity of the interpersonal focus was performed by analysing the effect of the average interpersonal tendency as suggested by Wiggins, Phillips, and Trapnell (1989) and by Gurtman (1991). The sample was divided into subgroups of patients showing their predominant interpersonal distress within the different octants of the circumplex model. The categories to which the patients were assigned were distributed roughly equally ($n = 93$–110). In Table 2.2, the mean changes related to aspects of personality, as measured by the Giessen Test, are shown across these interpersonal categories.

A descriptive analysis of the relationship between these categories and differences in the Giessen Test revealed that all groups improved on the "depression" and "social potency" scales. To test differences between the categories, univariate analyses of variance

Table 2.1. Prediction of change by individual IIP scores[a]

	"Social response"		"Dominance"		"Underlying mood (depression)"		"Permeability"		"Social impotency"	
	$\beta(u)$	$\beta(i)$	$\beta(u)$	$\beta(i)$	$\beta(u)$	$\beta(i)$	$\beta(u)$	$\beta(i)$	$\beta(u)$	$\beta(i)$
PA	−0.06	0.02	−0.32**	−0.31**	−0.06	−0.06	−0.01	−0.06	−0.04	−0.12*
BC	−0.10*	−0.05	−0.02	−0.01	0.03	0.02	0.08	0.12*	0.04	0.01
DE	−0.09	−0.03	−0.07	−0.15**	−0.12	−0.08	0.05	0.03	0.10	0.02
FG	−0.04	0.02	0.05	0.06	−0.08	−0.06	0.01	0.01	0.19**	0.02
HI	−0.12**	−0.10*	0.13*	0.00	0.04	0.03	−0.01	0.02	0.09	0.02
JK	−0.15*	−0.06	0.03	−0.04	0.09	0.06	0.02	0.08	0.06	0.01
LM	−0.05	0.01	0.03	−0.02	0.12	0.08	0.17**	0.16**	0.06	0.02
NO	0.01	0.06	−0.01	−0.10*	0.01	0.01	0.04	−0.04	−0.10	−0.13*
Mean	−0.07	−0.24**	−0.01	−0.16**	0.22**	0.23**	0.03	0.16**	0.07	0.15*
R	.33	.27	.33	.37	.17	.27	.16	.23	.19	.21
R²	.10	.08	.10	.12	.05	.08	.04	.06	.04	.05
F	17.30	22.92	19.66	17.68	27.25	27.25	19.66	6.84	18.71	12.00
p<	.001	.001	.001	.001	.001	.001	.001	.001	.001	.001

[a]All regression equations employed the stepwise procedure; the solution presented is based on the final model; all regression coefficients are standardized. $\beta(u)$ = β of unipsatized scale scores; $\beta(i)$ = β of ipsatized scale scores. *$p < .05$; **$p < .01$.

29

Table 2.2. Interpersonal focus and changes in the Giessen test

Scales	Interpersonal focus in the two-dimensional space								mean	F	p
	PA	BC	DE	FG	HI	JK	LM	NO			
Social response[a]	−0.49	−1.33	−1.71	−2.71	−2.51	−2.40	−1.31	1.79	−1.42	2.38	.021
Dominance[b]	−1.10	−2.45	0.67	2.11	2.72	2.84	0.65	−0.63	0.67	6.12	.000
Self-control[c]	−0.98	−0.07	0.75	−1.01	0.40	0.45	0.18	−0.41	−0.12	0.85	.547
Mood (depression)[d]	3.25	3.48	3.14	3.38	5.24	4.42	2.78	2.22	3.50	1.23	.284
Permeability[e]	1.09	1.03	0.11	0.95	2.04	2.62	1.38	−1.49	1.07	0.89	.533
Social potency[5]	2.18	1.22	3.49	5.98	4.80	2.76	1.96	1.71	3.03	2.85	.006

[a] Negative = patients received more positive feedback from others at discharge; [b] negative = patients were more flexible at discharge. [c] negative = patients had a higher self-control at discharge; [d] positive = a decrease in depressive mood; [e] positive = patients were less retentive and more self-disclosing or permeable at discharge; [f] positive = patients were more socially potent at discharge.

(ANOVAs) were performed (Table 2.2). On the "social potency" scale, the mean differences were found to be significant within the categories BC ("vindictive") and NO ("intrusive"), showing lower scores than FG ("socially avoidant") and HI ("unassertive").

All other scales showed differential effects in the eight categories. In part, these differences can be attributed to the fact that patients with an interpersonal focus on FG, HI, and JK ("socially avoidant", "unassertive", and "exploitable") obtained the highest scores on admission. However, some peculiar findings emerged. The mean differences were significant on the "social response" scale, revealing a higher social response in patients from all categories, in particular FG, HI, and JK, but a lower social response in the NO ("intrusive") category. This was the only category with lower scores on "permeability", indicating that patients assigned to this group were more reserved after treatment. The differences in this scale were, however, not statistically significant. Another finding, which was theoretically consistent, was that in patients from all categories of the upper octants, dominance as a personality trait decreased, whereas it increased in patients located in two of the lower octants. These findings underline those of the regression analyses, indicating that the interpersonal focus clarifies the spectrum of the deeper dimension of personality-related changes.

The impact of the interpersonal focus on changes in interpersonal problems

The interpersonal focus should be important in predicting not only various types of outcome, but also general change in interpersonal problems during treatment. Table 2.3 provides the change scores of interpersonal problems across the eight interpersonal categories.

Patients with an interpersonal focus in the lower octants showed the greatest decrease in interpersonal problems during treatment pertaining to the fact that their baseline scores were especially high (regression to the mean). The HI and JK categories displayed even more interpersonal disturbance related to being too autocratic at discharge. One would assume that changes in interpersonal problems should be highest in the interpersonal area that

Table 2.3. Interpersonal focus and changes in interpersonal problems

Changes in IIP scales[a]	Interpersonal focus in the two-dimensional space								F	p
	PA	BC	DE	FG	HI	JK	LM	NO		
PA	*0.24*	0.24	0.12	0.05	−0.17	−0.14	0.12	0.22	8.76	.001
BC	0.07	*0.12*	0.13	0.13	0.00	0.00	0.02	0.05	2.60	.01
DE	0.00	−0.08	*0.27*	0.23	0.12	0.03	0.02	0.05	10.18	.001
FG	0.10	0.26	0.51	*0.73*	0.63	0.53	0.12	0.18	12.23	.001
HI	0.00	0.00	0.34	0.55	*0.61*	0.72	0.38	0.11	10.88	.001
JK	0.11	0.00	0.00	0.27	0.51	*0.64*	0.42	0.11	5.40	.001
LM	0.21	0.00	0.12	0.23	0.38	0.54	*0.48*	0.23	7.15	.001
NO	0.25	0.16	−0.05	0.03	0.02	0.25	0.46	*0.36*	4.90	.001
Total	0.15	0.15	0.23	0.29	0.29	0.31	9.22	0.15	4.75	.001

[a] The scores are based on unipsatized scores.

a patient most sensitively perceives. It was possible to confirm this assumption in most categories. There were only two exceptions: patients from categories BC and DE did not show any obvious alterations in their most conflictual interpersonal problem areas. Patients with a focus on BC showed no changes in several interpersonal dimensions (for instance DE, HI, JK, LM). One might conclude that patients who have their interpersonal focus in the cold and vindictive area improve in terms of intrapsychic aspects as measured by the Giessen Test; however, they do not change their dismissive interpersonal stance.

Discussion

Psychodynamic group treatment is the core element of many treatment programmes within psychotherapeutic hospitals, at least in Germany. Nevertheless, it has been somewhat neglected in research. It is for this reason that a working group on inpatient group psychotherapy was founded, aiming to promote research within this field in several naturalistic studies. The studies summarized here mainly focused on the question as to whether interpersonal characteristics of patients treated in inpatient groups might be used to differentially predict treatment outcome on different levels.

One general conclusion that can be drawn from the three studies undertaken by the working group is that patients who are more susceptible to interpersonal problems at the beginning of their treatment (i.e. patients with higher total scores on the IIP) seem to derive more benefit from the psychodynamic treatment than do patients suffering less from interpersonal distress. This benefit is related to symptomatic changes as well as personality-related outcome measures (Giessen Test). In some ways this result might have been expected, since psychodynamic group treatment should specifically focus on interpersonal issues. Accordingly, patients who are already familiar with these problems (perhaps related to "psychological mindedness") should have a better outcome. Nevertheless, even expected results should be considered in planning treatment programmes. One potential conclusion to be drawn from this result might be to assign patients with lower scores in the IIP to other treatments or, at least, to provide additional treatments focusing on increasing interpersonal sensitivity.

Apart from this global result, differential analyses of the data from the study give some additional information regarding the benefit that patients derive from psychodynamic group work in terms of personality-related criteria: being too nonassertive, too socially avoidant, or too vindictive at admission increases the likelihood of receiving more positive feedback from the environment at the end of the treatment (as measured by the Giessen Test scale "social response"). Being too domineering at admission had a significant impact on being more flexible and accommodating at the end of treatment, while being too nonassertive on admission had a significant effect on being more dominant (Giessen Test scale "dominance"). Using the ipsatized scores in this regression, being too domineering, too intrusive, and too vindictive was highly predictive of being more flexible and less dominant at the end of treatment. Interpersonal problems related to being too nurturant were predictive of higher permeability or self-disclosure at the end of treatment. This finding is not consistent with expectations: in line with the assumptions based upon interpersonal theory, we would have expected patients whose interpersonal focus is related to nurturance to benefit from therapy by being more reserved at discharge. The finding that patients who complained about being too vindictive on admission were at the time of discharge more permeable or self-disclosing was, however, in line with our assumptions. Being too socially avoidant predicted higher social potency or an increased capacity to carry out one's own desires at the end of treatment. It is important to note that, using the ipsatized scores, interpersonal problems of being too domineering and too intrusive predicted higher *social impotence*.

Summarizing these findings, the significant contribution of the IIP scales in predicting change in the personality test underlines not only the construct validity of interpersonal problems (see Davies-Osterkamp & Kriebel, 1993) but also, in particular, its predictive validity. Both different conceptions of the interpersonal problem scales seem to have their own predictive potential. In general, the use of ipsatized scores more strongly emphasizes the upper octants, while the use of unipsatized scores increases the impact of the lower octants, probably because the scores on these scales showed the highest correlations with the IIP total score. One might conclude that using the unipsatized scores emphasizes more strongly the effects on interpersonal problems in their literal meaning, while the use of ipsatized scores stresses the interpersonal focus or tendency.

On the whole, the finding of Horowitz, Rosenberg, and Bartholomew (1993) that problems with friendly submissiveness seem to be more easily treated in dynamic psychotherapy than are problems with hostile dominance was not obtained in the setting of inpatient psychodynamic group therapy. Even though when simply looking at the unipsatized effects of the IIP scales one might reach the conclusion that patients with a focus on friendly submissiveness might benefit more from group therapy, this assumption cannot be confirmed on the basis of the ipsatized scores. There was no kind of interpersonal problem dimension that did not have any positive effect on treatment outcome. We interpret these results to conclude that in group therapy it might be possible to take specifically targeted action regardless of the type of interpersonal problems predominantly experienced by patients at the beginning of therapy. These actions were aimed at achieving a new perception or a more positive stance related to specific interpersonal problems in each individual in the group. The mutual interactions in group therapy may specifically offer a better reflection of interpersonal aspects of the self and others.

CHAPTER THREE

Investigating structural change in the process and outcome of psychoanalytic treatment: The Heidelberg–Berlin Study

Tilman Grande, Gerd Rudolf, Claudia Oberbracht, Thorsten Jakobsen, & Wolfram Keller

History, focus, and present state of the research project

In 1993 the Confederation of German Psychoanalysts [Deutsche Gesellschaft für Psychoanalyse, Psychotherapie, Psychosomatik und Tiefenpsychologie (DGPT)] decided to support research on long-term psychoanalytic therapy. The DGPT's plan was to study high-intensity long-term psychoanalyses in comparison with one-hour/week psychodynamic psychotherapies. In calling for research proposals, the DGPT's essential objective was to subject the effectiveness and efficiency of long-term therapies to empirical investigation and thus marshal arguments that could be deployed in the ongoing health-policy debate in Germany. However, its initiative also coincided with an existing interest on the part of psychoanalytic organizations to evaluate their own work and gain a deeper understanding of it with the aid of systematic research. Aside from the question of effectiveness, the call for projects was thus also guided by an internal interest in the investigation of the processes and specific change mechanisms activated by psychoanalytic treatments.

In taking up the DGPT's invitation, our considerations soon centred on the fundamental question of whether, in view of the present state of research and methodology, their demand for a research project on the psychoanalyses could, in fact, be satisfied. The most important problem related to the fact that the research instruments used so far, against the background of the so-called "dose-effect models" (Howard, Kopta, Krause & Orlinsky, 1986), had identified significant changes in the early phases of psychotherapeutic treatment but only minor effects during the further course of treatment. On the basis of studies indebted to this model, Grawe, Donati, and Bernauer (1994) queried the usefulness of long-term therapies and concluded that positive effects can only be expected from treatments of up to about 50 hours.

Our position on this is a very different one. We are convinced that the specific effects of psychoanalyses—which, as clinical experience shows, only materialize after long and intensive treatment—cannot be detected with the aid of conventional research instruments. These measuring instruments operate close to the surface, capturing above all symptomatic or behavioural characteristics (Grande & Jakobsen, 1998), whereas from a psychoanalytic point of view the essential changes take place at the level of personality structure—that is, in the course of the breakdown of pathological structures that have taken shape during an individual's development and the reorganization and/or reintegration of the pathogenic intrapsychic conflicts and vulnerabilities embodied in those structures. Such processes of restructuring, which in all probability can only be achieved by means of long-term analytical processes, can obviously not be registered by conventional change-assessment techniques (see Strupp, Schacht, & Henry, 1988). These considerations led us to conclude that a project dealing with the effectiveness of long-term psychoanalytic therapies could only be successful if a method were available to assess central personality structure from a psychoanalytic point of view.

To this end, in 1992 a research group was constituted involving 40 scientists and clinicians with a psychoanalytic background and from 12 different universities; within the framework of the project on an Operationalized Psychodynamic Diagnosis (OPD) system, the group developed instruments designed to remedy this situation (Arbeitsgruppe OPD, 1998). Four years' work led to a classification system for research, teaching, and practice based on psychoanalytic constructs and thus transcending the purely descriptive approach underlying the existing systems (ICD, DSM). The OPD instruments thus assume a central position in our research approach, which, towards the end of 1993, was presented to the DGPT in the form of a project proposal (Grande, Rudolf, & Oberbracht, 1997; Rudolf & Grande, 1997). The plan was evaluated by several independent experts and classified as suitable for responding to the issues posed by the DGPT's call for projects.

In 1997, after a preliminary study, we were able to begin work on the project and start collecting data in Heidelberg (research group: Rudolf, Grande, Oberbracht, Jakobsen) and in Berlin (Keller, Dilg, Stehle). By mid-2000, a total of 61 cases from Heidelberg and Berlin had been incorporated into the study; the average length of therapy was approximately two years. As recruitment is still in progress and the therapies are long-term in design, the study itself is not yet complete. Accordingly, the present chapter presents a discussion of the study design and the methods we have developed to measure structural change. We will exemplify this procedure with reference to observations made in the actual course of the psychoanalytic treatment of one particular patient. Furthermore, we report on the outcome of preliminary investigations (now complete) on the reliability and validity of this method.

Central to our investigation is the question of the specific quality of therapeutic change that takes place in intensive psychoanalytic treatment on the one hand, and in low-frequency psychodynamic therapies on the other. Our hypothesis is that there are qualitatively distinct forms of change that can be designated as "coping" in the one instance and "structural change" in the other. We assume that "structural changes" are more likely to occur in psychoanalyses, whereas in low-frequency therapies there is a greater probability of encountering changes of a "coping" kind. We also hope to show how these two types of change have been conceptualized and operationalized in the study. In the final section of this chapter we return to this distinction and refine our hypothesis with reference to the investigatory methods we employed.

Study design, sample, and research instruments

Figure 3.1 shows the study design. It involves 30 patients receiving psychoanalytic psychotherapy of at least three hours a week and 30 psychotherapy patients in a one-hour sedentary setting. To protect this number of cases against attrition, 36 patients are admitted to each group. At the outset of therapy, the patients are subjected to detailed diagnostic examination; assessments are then made at three- or six-monthly intervals until treatment termination. Recent research by Sandell, Blomberg, and Lazar (1999) strongly suggests that frequency and setting differences have their clearest effects in the years following the termination of therapy. Accordingly, a further central line of inquiry examines the changes taking place in that period, and hence the research design also extends to follow-up studies, which are to take place one and three years after the termination of therapy.

The patients admitted to the study display severe neurotic, psychosomatic, and personality disorders. In our study patients are classified as severely disordered if they present a moderate or low integration level on the "structure" axis of the OPD (see below) and, in addition, display clear-cut symptoms measured by an Impairment Severity Score (Schepank, 1995). The patients are assessed on the basis of these criteria before admission. With an eye to ensuring continuous comparability of the differential effects in

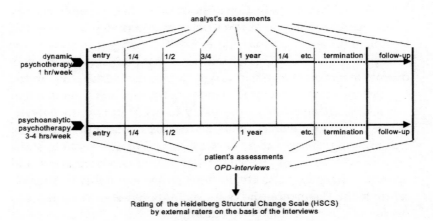

Figure 3.1. Study design.

the two groups, each of the participating analysts brings to the project one psychoanalytic case and one psychotherapy case. In this way possible confounding factors associated with the person of the analyst are compensated for in both groups.

The two treatment groups are matched for sex, age, educational level, and disorder severity (using the above-mentioned inclusion criteria), so that some level of patient comparability is also assured. The alternative—of employing randomized group allocation—is hardly feasible under normal outpatient conditions and carries its own substantial scientific risks regarding the validity of the investigation (by distorting the object of study). Hence a decision was made in favour of a naturalistic design plus subsequent group matching. In many other details of the study care is also taken to ensure protection of the therapeutic situation and as little interference from our research as possible. For example, the data-collection procedure is organized in such a way that analyst and patient negotiate involvement in the study before the onset of therapy but not in the course of it. Where a degree of research impact on therapeutic work is unavoidable, this is documented both by the external raters and by the analysts and is incorporated in the evaluation.

The data collected in the course and at the end of therapy stem from four different observational vantage points: patient self-assessment, analyst assessment, health insurance data, and assessments by external raters (see Grande, Rudolf, & Oberbracht, 1997). The following is an (incomplete) overview of the instruments used and the domains captured by these assessments.

1. *Patient self-assessment:*   data are collected at the beginning and in the course of therapy on social status, socio-demographic factors, health and health behaviour (items from the Berlin Jung study and the Berlin psychotherapy study: see Keller, Dilg, Westhoff, Rohner, & Studt, 1997; Rudolf, 1991a); SCL–90–R (Derogatis, Lipman, & Covi, 1975); Psychic and Social-Communicative Questionnaire (PSKB–Se) (Rudolf, 1991b); IIP (Horowitz, Strauss, & Kordy, 1994); Mental Health Scale (SG Scale from the TPF) (Becker, 1989); Introject questionnaire of the Structural Analysis of Social Behaviour (SASB) (Benjamin, 1974; Tress, 1993).

2. *Analyst assessment—at the outset and at termination:*   ICD–10 diagnoses (Dilling, Mombour, & Schmidt, 1991); conflicts, structural level, severity of impairment (short version of OPD); Initial Working Alliance (iTAB) (Grande, Porsch, & Rudolf, 1988; Rudolf, 1991a); physical symptoms and psychic symptoms (Heidelberg Documentation System) (Rudolf, Laszig, & Henningsen, 1997).

   Analyst assessment—in the course of therapy: information on setting and interruptions; significance of and changes in symptomatology over the preceding three months (free description); analytic process and cooperation, contents and themes in the therapeutic work (free description); session protocols; Therapeutic Working Alliance (TAB) (Grande, Porsch, & Rudolf, 1988; Rudolf, 1991a).

3. *Health insurance data:*   number of days in hospital, sick leave, use of medical services three years prior to therapy and three years after termination of therapy; data provided by the health insurance institutions.

4. *Assessment by external raters:*   OPD rating, focus selection, and HSCS (Heidelberg Structural Change Scale) rating in the course of treatment based on videotaped interviews (explained in detail below).

The last of these lines of inquiry is a special feature of our study, given that the use of external observers is unusual in connection with psychoanalytic therapies. Virtually all other existing studies limit themselves to assessments by patients and/or analysts, thus foregoing the independent and hence more objective judgement of external observers. The rationale for this is based on concern that the psychoanalytic process might be impaired by third-person involvement. Some studies draw on tape recordings of sessions, but these cannot provide information matching the quality of clinical interviews where the degree of change achieved is subjected to systematic verification. In our study, clinical interviews carried out at regular intervals in the course of treatment by external assessors supply the material for the subsequent assessment of process and outcome by independent raters. This feature sets the study apart from existing empirical psychoanalytic research and represents one of its main methodological specialities.

The number of patients ($n = 30$ for each group) may appear small in terms of statistical power compared with the methods usually used to measure therapeutic outcome and differential treatment effects. But the drawbacks of a small number of cases can be compensated for by specific hypotheses concerning the differences between the two forms of therapy and the use of instruments sensitive enough to capture those differences. In the study this is achieved by the use of instruments specifically designed for the psychoanalytic approach, notably the Structural Change Scale (see below).

In addition, restricting the study to a relatively small number of cases means that the use of time-consuming study procedures becomes a viable proposition. For example, the rating of one single videotaped interview takes, on average, 16 hours; the number of interviews per analysis can be anything from six to twelve or more, depending on the length of the treatment. No less time-consuming are the qualitative text evaluation procedures used to study the written reports of the analysts on the course of therapy. The material thus gathered is so extensive and detailed as to make individual case studies feasible over and above the findings on the groups.

An OPD-based procedure for measuring change

Operationalized Psychodynamic Diagnosis system

We have already indicated the major significance of the methods developed by the OPD Study Group for the investigation of the process and the effects of psychoanalytic treatment. The OPD (Arbeitsgruppe OPD, 1998) encompasses *five axes*, of which three are *psychodynamic* in the stricter sense of the term: those pertaining to "relationship" (Axis II), "conflict" (Axis III), and "structure" (Axis IV). The other two axes assess illness-related behaviour with respect to the preconditions of treatment (motivation, resources, etc.) and psychiatric disorders in accordance with the *International Classification of Diseases* (ICD–10; Dilling, Mombour, & Schmidt, 1991). For the study design envisaged here, only the three psychodynamic axes are relevant.

1. *The OPD Relationship Axis:*   The *Relationship Diagnosis* identi-
    fies the core dysfunctional relationship pattern displayed by a
    patient. Integral to this pattern are interpersonal behaviours
    and positions taken up by the *patient* and his/her *objects* in the
    core problematic relational constellation repeatedly established
    by the patient. The specific quality of these positions and the
    relational behaviour associated with them is described for each
    patient individually with reference to a given list of 30 items.

    a. The first step is to map the pattern from the *subjective experi-
    ential perspective of the patient.* Here we draw on relationship
    episodes reported by the patient in the course of the interview:
    these allow conclusions to be drawn about the internal ideas
    and perceptions entertained by the patient in connection with
    the problems he/she has in handling interpersonal relation-
    ships.

    b. The second stage is to describe the pattern from the *subjective
    experiential perspective of others* (including the interviewer). Here
    we draw additionally on the relational behaviour of the patient
    in the interview itself, with the countertransference of the
    interviewer figuring as a source of information

    c. The third stage integrates the two experiential viewpoints
    into a single *relation-dynamic formulation,* combining the results
    of the first two stages to form a cogent relational gestalt (for
    greater detail see Grande et al., 1997).

2. *The OPD Conflict Axis:*   Within the framework of *Conflict Diag-
    nosis,* eight conflict types are defined as having a potentially
    crucial effect on the lives of the patients. The scaling is used to
    assess how significant each of these conflicts is for the indi-
    vidual patient. The types of conflict encompassed are: *depend-
    ency versus autonomy, submission versus control, need for care
    versus self-sufficiency, self-esteem conflicts, superego and guilt con-
    flicts, oedipal–sexual conflicts, identity conflicts*; also included is
    the clinical syndrome described as *deficient awareness of feelings
    and conflicts.* The manual describes criteria for the elaboration of
    these conflicts in the following areas: partner selection, attach-
    ment behaviour/family life, family of origin, behaviour in the
    vocational/professional sphere, behaviour in the socio-cultural

environment, and illness behaviour. A four-tier scale is used to assess whether and with what degree of intensity a conflict is present. In addition, raters are instructed to indicate which two of these conflicts are most important for the patient. A concluding assessment records whether the patient's handling of the conflicts corresponds to a more active or passive mode.

3. *The OPD Structure Axis:* In *Structure Diagnosis*, the patient's level of functioning and integration is assessed on the basis of the structural capacities and vulnerabilities displayed in terms of six dimensions. These dimensions record capacities for *self-awareness, self-regulation, defence, object awareness, communication*, and *attachment*. They are used to assess the patient's *level of integration,* using the ratings "well integrated", "moderately well integrated", "poorly integrated", and "disintegrated". The criteria for these ratings are defined in the manual for all dimensions. In a final assessment, structure is given a global rating, on the same four-level basis. As Table 3.1 shows, each of the six dimensions has a number of sub-dimensions identifying the various aspects of the superordinate structural capacity in question. For example, the *"capacity for self-regulation"* dimension encompasses the sub-dimensions "tolerance of affects", "regulation of self-esteem", "regulation of impulses", and "anticipation" (Rudolf, Oberbracht, & Grande, 1998).

Considerations bearing upon the use of the OPD

As noted above, the usual devices for measuring change define improvements in the course of therapy in terms of the gradual alleviation of pathology (symptoms). In the case of the OPD, however, this model has only limited significance. There are three reasons for this:

1. Studies on 12-week inpatient therapies (Grande, Rudolf, & Oberbracht, 2000) have shown that OPD findings are relatively stable over time and show very little change in relatively brief therapies. This is scarcely surprising if we remember that the OPD is designed to capture difficulties located at a deeper level

Table 3.1. OPD axes and focus list

Relationship

Individualized formulation of a core dysfunctional relationship pattern

Life-determining conflicts

1. Dependence/autonomy conflict
2. Submission/control conflict
3. Care/self-sufficiency conflict
4. Self-value conflicts

5. Guilt conflicts
6. Oedipal-sexual conflicts
7. Identity conflicts
8. Deficient awareness of feelings and conflicts

Structural capacities/vulnerabilities

1. Capacity for experience of self
   - self-reflection
   - image of self
   - identity
   - differentiation of affects
2. Capacity for self-regulation
   - affect-tolerance· contact
   - regulation of self-esteem
   - regulation of impulses
   - anticipation
3. Capacity for defence
   - intrapsychic defenses
   - flexibility

4. Capacity for object-experience
   - self-object differentiation
   - empathy
   - awareness of total objects
   - object-related affects
5. Capacity for communication

   - decoding other's affects
   - encoding own affects
   - reciprocity
6. Capacity for attachment
   - internalizations
   - detaching
   - variability of relationships

---

in the patient's personality and hence less easy to change than are symptoms or symptomatic behaviour (see Grande & Jakobsen, 1998; Schulte, 1995).

2. In findings of a psychodynamic nature the model of therapeutic "improvement" of pathological conditions has only limited relevance, because here change does not take place in terms of "more" or "less" but, rather, along the lines of a qualitative reshaping or an enhanced integration of problematic aspects of the OPD profile. In the successful course of an analytic process

a patient's central conflicts are not neutralized; it would be more accurate to say that they are constructively modified and better integrated in the important spheres of life. Nor does the central problematic relationship pattern become "diminished" in the course of a successful therapy; what happens instead is that it loses more and more of its compulsive character, involves less subjective suffering for the patient, and is recast in qualitative terms.

With respect to the structural vulnerabilities of the type identified in the "structure" axis of the OPD, it would be more fitting to regard improvement in terms of the disappearance or reduction of pathological abnormalities. For example, in the course of successful treatment a patient's affect tolerance or self–object differentiation may change, and this change may, indeed, be reflected in the rating scores. But here, too, it often seems clinically more appropriate, in the case of therapeutic success, to speak of an enhanced integration of certain vulnerabilities, which by no means implies that the latter have simply vanished as a theme in the patient's life.

3. A further problem is that for individual patients not all the sections of the OPD profile may be equally relevant in change terms. There are always a small number of pathogenic conflicts and structural vulnerabilities that are especially significant for the specific problems of a given patient. Frequently, other abnormalities can be interpreted as secondary repercussions of these central problem areas. This small set of individually crucial areas can be regarded as nodal points in a network of dynamic interrelations on which other problems depend. They thus represent basal reference points for any treatment aiming at substantial therapeutic change.

The focus concept

A technique for measuring change on the basis of the OPD must be designed in such a way as to take due conceptual account of the difficulties listed above. In our study we do this by defining *change as restructuring in the sense of a growing integration of specific problem areas that are of central significance for a patient's psychodynamics.* We assume that for every patient it is possible to define a limited number of such specific problems that can be used to observe therapeutic change. We also refer to these problem areas as "foci", but it is essential to note that in the present context these are *research foci,* not therapeutic foci, in contrast to normal parlance.

The selection of these foci is undertaken via expert assessment by the external raters (Figure 3.1). The problem areas rated here as foci are those that are presumed to sustain both the patient's psychic/psychosomatic symptoms and his/her interpersonal problems. One problem area from the OPD spectrum is judged as being central and selected as a focus, in the sense that here something will have to change if the patient's problems are to be alleviated or dispelled. Defining the foci, therefore, is in the nature of establishing a case-related psychodynamic hypothesis specifying a patient's change-relevant characteristics.

Technically the procedure is that for each patient five central problems are selected from the OPD "relationship", "conflicts", and "structure" sectors. This choice is based on the range of 30 potential problem areas listed in Table 3.1. These areas derive from the core dysfunctional relationship pattern, the eight conflicts, and the 21 subdimensions from the "structure" axis. In former studies (Grande, Rudolf & Oberbracht, 2000) we have established that the selection of five foci is sufficient to home in on the most important aspects of a patient's psychodynamic constitution. These studies have also demonstrated that in every case the habitual dysfunctional relationship pattern should be defined as one of the foci. The remaining problems are selected from the "conflict" and "structure" areas, with the proviso that at least one problem area be selected from each of these axes. Thus the selection of foci can be weighted in favour of conflicts or structural vulnerabilities, depending on the severity of the structural impairment displayed by a given patient. This reflects clinical experience of the way in which, depending on the nature and severity of an impairment, the diagnosis and treatment of each patient will place greater emphasis either on structural features or on unconscious conflicts.

The Heidelberg Structural Change Scale

After selecting the foci, the next step is to assess the state of therapeutic change the patient has reached with regard to these problem areas. For this purpose we use a modified form of the Assimilation of Problematic Experiences Scale (APES) by Stiles, Meshot, Anderson, and Sloan (1992). This scale enables us to describe more subtle changes in a patient's dealings with given structural problems. The term "assimilation" here designates, with reference to Piaget, a process in which difficult experiences are acquired, integrated, and reshaped. The authors themselves conceptualize this process as being free of theoretical biases or allegiance to any specific therapeutic orientation. We have revised APES with an eye to more closely assimilating it to the exigencies of psychoanalytic treatment (Rudolf, Grande, & Oberbracht, 2000). The revision is in line with the logic set out in Freud's 1914 study "Remembering, Repeating and Working-Through". Our modifications of APES are extensive, and hence we refer to this instrument as the *Heidelberg Structural Change Scale* (Figure 3.2).

Each stage of the scale marks a therapeutically significant step, beginning with the increasing awareness of a problem area that had not been perceived as such until then, extending through to the therapeutic working-through of the aspects and experiences associated with it, and from there to more basic changes resulting from it, both in the patient's experience and in his/her concrete external behaviour. With the aid of the scale, patients are assessed as to the degree of structural change they have achieved at a given point in their treatment. A separate assessment is made on the scale for each of the five foci defined.

Figure 3.3 gives an overview of the stages in the measurement of structural change. At the outset of therapy a semi-structured videotaped OPD interview (Janssen et al., 1996) is used to rate the OPD, to select the five focal problems from the OPD focus list, and to assess the patient's ability to deal with these foci in terms of the HSCS. At each new rating time-point the five foci are re-assessed with respect to the HSCS on the basis of new interviews, thus pinpointing the progress of restructuring within the separate focal areas. Two raters work independently at each stage of this rating process. After completion they are asked to arrive at a consensus

STAGES		EXCERPT FROM THE MANUAL
1. *Focus problem warded off*	exact **1** match **1+** tendency↓	The problem is completely unconscious; experiences connected with it are evaded; problematic behavior is ego-syntonic; the patient has "no problems" with the critical area
2. *Unwanted preoccupation with the focus*	tendency↑ **2-** exact **2** match **2+** tendency↓	Unpleasant feelings and thoughts in connection with the problem area can no longer be immediately rejected; but preoccupation with the problem is reluctant; external confrontations with the problem take place but are rejected as disturbances; no realisation that the problems might be associated with the patient's own person
3. *Vague awareness of the focus*	Tendency↑ **3-** exact **3** match **3+** tendency↓	Patient notices/suspects the existence of a problem that is part of him/herself and cannot simply be rejected; in the course of repetition the problem takes on a continuing existence; negative affects originate from the tension between the insistent nature of the problem and the patient's defensive/aversive attitude
4. *Acceptance and exploration of the focus*	tendency↑ **4-** exact **4** match **4+** tendency↓	The problem starts to take on a new shape in the patient's consciousness; incipient indications of an active, "head-on" preoccupation with it; the problem can now be formulated as an "assignment" and hence be made the subject of therapeutic work; destructive, rejecting responses may interfere with this attitude but can no longer undermine it altogether
5. *Deconstruction in the focus area*	tendency↑ **5-** exact **5** match **5+** tendency↓	Querying and disintegration of accustomed coping modes; uncertainty about evaluations of own person and others; perception of own limitations and deficiencies; resignation and moods of despair alternate with urges toward reparation; old modes are lost and cut off, new ones not yet accessible
6. *Reorganization in the focus area*	tendency↑ **6-** exact **6** match **6+** tendency↓	Abandonment and final relinquishing of accustomed coping modes; in his/her own experience patient is increasingly self-reliant and able to take in hand and assume responsibility for his/her own life in the problem area; increasingly conciliatory approach to problem area; problem solutions spontaneous and unexpected; re-integration
7. *Integration of the focus problem*	tendency↑ **7-** exact **7** match	Dealing with the problem has become something natural; the area has lost its special significance in the eyes of the patient; the problem is something belonging to the past, preoccupying patient - as a memory

Figure 3.2. The Heidelberg Structural Change Scale (HSCS).

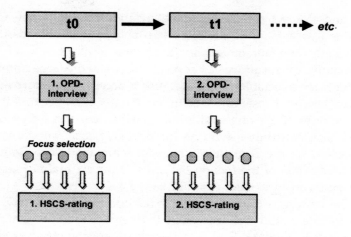

Figure 3.3. Overview of stages in measurement of structural change.

rating on the basis of their independent judgements and to record this in a written commentary, thus producing a brief description of the level of therapeutic progress achieved for each of the focal areas. Table 3.3 and Figure 3.9 (for comments on this case see below) give an example of the way the therapeutic changes for the five foci of an individual patient are recorded on the HSCS.

Reliability and validity

Investigations of the reliability of the method described here were undertaken in the framework of a study on inpatient therapy for patients with psychosomatic, neurotic, and personality disorders (Rudolf, Grande, Oberbracht, & Jakobsen, 1996). We draw further material from the cases within the ongoing study reported on in the present chapter. The scores set out below are based on calculations collating data from both studies.

For the HSCS we have established interrater agreement of $r = .77$ (Pearson correlation) on the basis of $N = 306$ individual focus ratings. The reliability test for *focus selection* refers only to the four foci selected from the OPD sectors "conflict" and "structure" (Axes

III and IV). As the dysfunctional relationship pattern was pre-defined as a focus in all cases (see above) it is not possible to calculate rater agreement on it. On the basis of $N = 161$ focus selections, the result was a kappa of .59. Given the large number of potentially selectable foci, this figure is acceptable. It corresponds to a relatively conservative estimate of agreement because it takes no account of existing similarities between the foci *within* the six OPD Structure dimensions. As Table 3.1 shows, the subdimensions allocated to the Structure dimensions are relatively similar. A categorization of the foci on the basis of the six main dimensions produces an agreement result of kappa = .70.

Indications of the validity of the method can also be drawn from the inpatient study referred to. With reference to a study involving 49 patients, Grande, Rudolf, Oberbracht, and Jakobsen (2001) report that the pre/post differences averaged for all five foci of a given patient show a high correlation with the global outcome assessments of various members of the therapeutic team. As Table 3.2 shows, these correlations vary between .43 and .50. No other scale of change in this study had a higher degree of correlation with the global outcome. Indeed, the correlation between these assessments and the symptom change measurements "somatization" (SOM), "depression" (DEP), "social anxiety" (SA), and "somatic anxiety symptoms" (SoA) was lower throughout (pre-post differences of the PSKB–Se (Rudolf, 1991b).

Table 3.2. The HSCS in relation to different assessments of therapeutic success

Pre-post differences of . . .	Global assessments of therapeutic success by . . .		
	Therapist	Therapeutic rounds	Staff
HSCS	.50**	.47**	.43*
Somatization	.49**	.34*	.35
Depression	.42**	.27	.26
Social anxiety	.30	.11	.29
Somatic anxiety symptoms	.27	.25	.14

*$p < .05$; $p < .01$. N = max. 49 because of missing data.

These findings justify the conclusion that, taken in isolation, symptomatic changes do not suffice to capture what clinicians regard as therapeutic success. The study shows that the focus-related changes measured with HSCS map the global outcome of the treatment with greater clinical accuracy. This may have to do with the fact that clinicians (of a psychodynamic persuasion) do not rely on symptom improvement alone when assessing treatment success but inquire whether and to what extent patients have mode progress in the working-through of their central problem areas. Clinicians may have greater confidence in this form of therapeutic progress because it represents a sounder basis for further development after completion of therapy.

That this is indeed the case is borne out by the six-month follow-up study by Grande, Rudolf, Oberbracht, and Pauli-Magnus (2003) on 39 patients from the same study. It showed that patients with a high score on the HSCS (averaged across five foci) at the end of therapy did better after discharge. The analysis of significant events in the lives of patients after inpatient treatment indicated that coping with those events was more adaptive if the patient had achieved improved HSCS scores in the course of therapy (highly significant correlation of .42). This can be interpreted as meaning that patients were better able to cope with the demands placed on them by their home lives if they had gained an awareness of the problematic tendencies interfering with their coping efforts in those areas. The study also demonstrates that this is not possible before Stages 3 or 4 on the scale, when perception and/or acknowledgment of the focus problem has been achieved (Figure 3.2).

These findings show that the HSCS can be used reliably and maps changes at a good level of agreement with the assessment of therapy success by clinical experts. They also strongly suggest that improvements on the HSCS correlate with patients' increasing ability to regulate and cope with problem-related demands placed on them in their home lives. All in all, then, these studies supply evidence that the HSCS is an instrument that can be used to measure changes at a deeper level than the merely symptomatic. In the next section we take an individual instance of psychoanalytic psychotherapy to show how structural changes can be measured with this instrument.

A case study

The patient, Mr B: clinical data

Mr B, 22 years old, responded to his girlfriend's termination of their relationship with depression and suicidal leanings. He had been subdepressive for a number of years before that and suffered from social anxieties impairing his career prospects. In the presence of others he regularly felt pressured and reacted with a markedly vegetative symptomatology. In compensation he cultivated notions in which he fantasized about being equipped with unusual intellectual abilities and artistic potential. After his parents' separation early in his life, the patient grew up with his mother. His dependency on her was intensive and ambivalent. Despite their many conflicts, he was hardly able to live a life of his own. He had occasional contact with his father, of whom he was critical but whom he also painfully missed.

According to ICD–10 this was classified as a depressive episode (F32.1) and a social phobia (F40.1). The following five problem areas from the OPD profile were established as foci for the patient: (1) the dysfunctional, maladaptive relationship pattern; (2) sexual/oedipal conflicts; (3) regulation of self-esteem; (4) contact; and (5) detachment (3 to 5 from the "structure" axis).

After separation, the patient embarked on a course of psychoanalytic psychotherapy involving three hours a week with a male analyst (recumbent). After 2½ years and approximately 280 sessions, the therapy is now over, and the data from it are available in their entirety. The follow-up studies have yet to ensue. The following delineates the course and the outcome of this treatment as reflected in the patient's self-assessment and the external examiners' ratings. The scales and assessment instruments used in the charting of the case were:

1. symptom changes mapped by three PSKB–Se Scales (Psychic and Social-Communicative Questionnaire, self-assessment version; Rudolf, 1991b): "somatic anxiety symptoms", "depression", and "somatization";

2. Inventory of Interpersonal Problems (IIP–D: German version) (Horowitz, Strauss, & Kordy, 1994);

3. Heidelberg Structural Change Scale;

4. freely formulated clinical observations by the external raters on the selected "detaching" focus (5) and the changes discernible in the course of therapy.

Naturally the documentation of this case as given here is not complete, because a large number of additional data have not been taken into account. We refrain from alluding to the psychoanalyst's perspective and his assessment of the analytic process. We also ignore the health insurance data and what they tell us about the cost of the medical services provided and the number of days the patient was off work because of his illness. Instead. we limit our view to the assessments listed in order to obtain a clearer picture of the ratio of symptomatic and structural changes displayed by Mr B. In so doing we are also preparing the ground for a later section, where we take a closer look at the relationship between psycho-therapeutic and psychoanalytic treatment effects and refine the central hypothesis underlying this study.

Self-assessments of Mr B

Figure 3.4 shows the progress of the symptomatology over the first two years of psychoanalysis, measured on the "somatic anxiety symptoms", "depression", and "somatization" scales taken from the PSKB–Se (Rudolf, 1991b). The ratings are expressed as T-values; scores below 60 can be regarded as clinically "normal". The figure shows a drop in the initially very high symptom scores to a normal range after a period of between six months and one year; thereafter we have a reactivation of the symptomatology to a clinically abnormal score after two years from the start of treat-ment. This applies notably to the "depression" and "somatic anxi-ety symptoms" scales. But after this temporary rise, the scores on both scales ultimately return to the clinically normal range.

We find a very similar curve for the "over-introverted", "over-exploitable", and "over-submissive" scales and for the IIP–D (Horowitz, Strauss, & Kordy, 1994), where the patient again had a

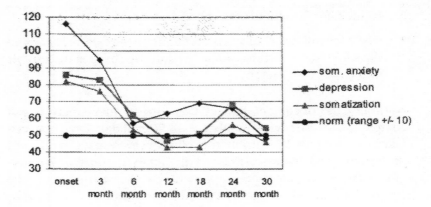

Figure 3.4. Symptom change in the course of treatment.

fairly high score at the outset (Figure 3.5). Here the reactivation trend in the second year of treatment was even more marked. But again we have a reduction of interpersonal problems towards the end of therapy. Finally, the same course can be seen in Figure 3.6, which shows the graph of the IIP total score.

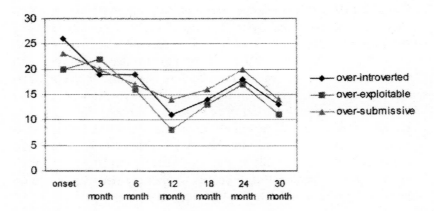

Figure 3.5. IIP scales "over-introverted", "over-exploitable", and "over-submissive".

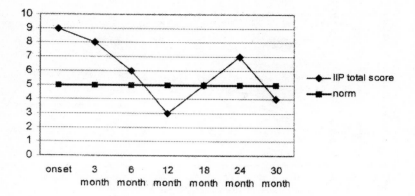

Figure 3.6. IIP total score (stanine values).

Comments and ratings
by the external independent examiners

Figures 3.7 and 3.8 show the development of the patient from the perspective of the external raters assessing the changes in the five focus areas on the basis of videotaped OPD interviews and using the HSCS. The figures show the scores for the individual foci in the course of time. The scores for "relationship pattern", "detachment" (Figure 3.7), and "contact" (Figure 3.8) show continuous improvement and by the end of treatment are in fact very good. The "oedipal–sexual conflicts" (Figure 3.7) and "regulation of self-esteem" (Figure 3.8) focus areas also show improvement but after one year remain constant at Stage 4 of the "acceptance and exploration of the focus" scale. Of note is the fact that after 1½ and 2 years of therapy the patient had reached Stage 5 "deconstruction in the focus area" first for one (Figure 3.7: "detaching", score 5–) and then for two ("relationship" and "oedipal–sexual conflicts", scores 5– and 5) focal areas. The Manual (see abridged version in Figure 3.2) speaks in this connection of uncertainty, resignation and despair, perception and ultimate acknowledgment of the patient's own limitations and impairments, and depressive affects bound up with this.

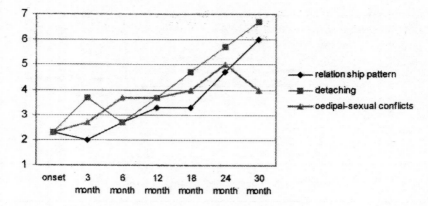

Figure 3.7. HSCS rating for the foci "relationship", "oedipal–sexual conflicts", and "detaching".

As mentioned earlier, after their HSCS rating the external examiners set down a detailed commentary in which the specific form taken by the focal areas and the focal changes are described with reference to the contents of the interviews. These commentaries have the advantage of providing a readily usable clinical impression of the patient and the therapy. Table 3.3 shows a condensed version of these commentaries for one of Mr B's focal problems. The focus in question is "detaching", figuring in the focus list (Figure 3.3) as a structural capacity/vulnerability and

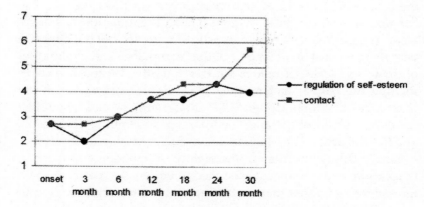

Figure 3.8. HSCS rating for the foci "regulation of self-esteem" and "contact".

allocated to the OPD structure dimension "attachment". We see here a development in which over the period of 2½ years the patient moves through a defensive/anxious and at the same time aggressive distancing from the object to a more intensive involvement accompanied by ambivalence and feelings of depression;

Table 3.3. External raters' commentaries on development in focal area "detaching" (condensed version)

	HSCS score	Patient's management of focus problem
Onset	2+	Despair, depression and thoughts of suicide following separation from girlfriend; inability to live a life of his own; responsibility for this attributed to mother
3 months	4–	First rift in the union with the mother through realization that she will die some time; acknowledgment of having a part in this dependence; purchase of own washing-machine; twin-like relationship with a friend
6 months	3–	Engagement with the focal problem has become vaguer again, much acting-out in this connection; first meeting with father; welcomes analysis break because of fear of dependence on analyst
1 year	4–	Reflection on his "fateful union" with the mother; hate and conciliatory reports on the mother, more differentiated, three-dimensional description of mother; interest in sexuality and own attractiveness; loosening of bonds with friend, more clearly delimited relationship; first emphasis of autonomy vis-à-vis interviewer
1.5 years	5–	Mourning over contradictory relationship with mother and guilt feelings; disappointed at relationship with father; feels wrongly treated in the analysis; makes indirect accusations in OPD interview (dryness of mouth!); expresses longing for a girlfriend
2 years	6–	Conciliatory moods where, though regretting what his mother was unable to give, he shows understanding for the restrictions she placed on him and takes a caring view of this; only very occasional defiant bids for delimitation; new self-assurance with regard to own abilities and potential; feels more autonomous
2.5 years	7–	Is able to empathize with mother and support her without worrying about self-delimitation; is also able to accept support from another woman; is in love again; feels enterprising and autonomous.

subsequently a genuine detachment takes place, in the aftermath of which the patient can draw on a sound degree of autonomy and can, for that reason, afford without risk to seek close relations with the objects and open out to them.

Synopsis of the case

We can summarize the course taken by our case example on the various observation levels as follows: in the first year the patient develops from a more reluctant engagement with his problem areas (Stage 2 of the HSCS, Figure 3.2) to active acknowledgment and exploration of his problems (Stage 4). During this period the somatic, psychic, and interpersonal complaints disappear almost completely. At the beginning of the second year of therapy we see a qualitative difference. The patient experiences his problems more intensively. On the basis of the more firmly established therapeutic relationship he now ventures to, as it were, expose himself to them. At the symptom level this goes hand and hand with a moderate reactivation of symptomatology and a clear increase in the inter-personal difficulties experienced by the patient. A phase of more intensive analytic working-through has begun, which we allocate to Stage 5 ("deconstruction in the focus area") on the HSCS. Only after this phase of instability do the changes set in that in clinical terms appear soundly "organic" and firmly rooted, thus promising to be more than temporary. The follow-up will show whether this interpretation is valid.

Structural and psychotherapeutic changes

In our discussion of the case example of Mr B, Stage 5 on the HSCS and the temporarily destabilizing processes bound up with it mark a caesura allowing a distinction between the effects of psychothera-pies and psychoanalyses in terms of ideal types. Clinical experi-ence shows that in psychoanalyses external changes may take a long time to materialize, appearing spontaneously at a later date when a solution has had sufficient time to mature inwardly. In

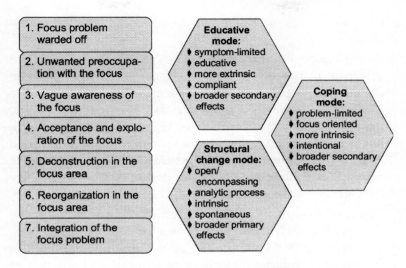

Figure 3.9. Modes of therapeutic change.

terms of the process model we have developed, this occurs at Stages 6 and 7 when old, consolidated defence or coping structures have disintegrated (Stage 5).

The spontaneous character of changes deriving from an analytic process is quite conceivably one feature that clearly distinguishes psychoanalyses from other forms of psychotherapeutic treatment aiming at a specific therapeutic change either via focusing or direct educative intervention. Figure 3.9 shows how various modes of change can be allocated to certain sections of the HSCS.

1. *Educative mode:*   At Stages 1 and 2 of the scale, positive changes are most likely to be achieved if the therapeutic approach is symptom-related and educative. Here the patient is more extrinsically motivated in his attempts to bring about change and—in productive instances—behaves in a compliant, cooperative way. Correspondingly, the changes themselves are symptom-related. At a secondary level, however, the decrease of symptomatic impairment can definitely trigger notable other effects—for example, via a gain in the subjective awareness of personal competence and an improvement in self-esteem, which may, in its turn, then generate further favourable effects

of a nature not necessarily specific to the intentions of the therapy.

2. *Coping mode:*   Distinct from this is a coping mode where the therapeutic approach is geared to the inner psychic problem domain connected with the symptomatology and sets out to uncover this focally. With this approach, patients' insight into their own problem enables them to attain greater ability to manage their own problems in the form of conscious regulation and to bring about change via intentional endeavour. Here the motivation is more intrinsic. From this mode broader positive effects may derive, as described above (coping mode).

3. *Structural change mode:*   The third mode is that of structural change proper. Here the therapeutic approach is basically open and characterized by the willingness of the therapist to take comprehensive account of the personality of the patient in its conscious/unconscious forms of expression and to allow for an analytic process. Here again, the patient's changes are intrinsically motivated; however, essentially they are not consciously desired but transpire spontaneously, sometimes surprising the patients themselves. The effects triggered by this mode are primarily broad in scope and at the same time specific to the equally broad therapeutic intention.

It needs to be stressed that these modes can by no means be paired off with therapy techniques in a clear-cut manner. Within behavioural therapy, for example, there are techniques that would certainly qualify for inclusion in the coping mode. Equally, certain intrinsically psychodynamic therapies may display educative elements or in certain cases initiate an analytic process, even though the setting does not comply with the classical requirements. For this reason, the change modes in the figure are allocated to the stages on the scale in a way intended to be approximate and overlapping.

In principle, however, our working hypothesis for the study as a whole is that in psychoanalysis there is a higher incidence of developments corresponding to the third change mode (structural change) and described by Stages 5 to 7 on the HSCS . For psychotherapies, on the other hand, we expect a higher frequency of changes at Stages 3 and 4, and corresponding to the coping mode. This specific hypothesis is the central distinctive assumption of the study and will be subjected to statistical verification via comparison between the groups.

We anticipate that this approach will do more than merely furnish global evidence for the superiority of one therapy form over another. We expect it to supply a better understanding of the way in which various different processes achieve their effects and of the processes they set in train, and the likelihood not only of a good sustainable therapy outcome but also of the risks of standstill and failure. The structural change model developed by the authors and condensed in the scale represents a viable method of imaging change processes beyond the symptom level and hence of capturing the specific outcomes traceable to psychoanalysis in the therapeutic change process.

CHAPTER FOUR

Contribution to the measurement of mode-specific effects in long-term psychoanalytic psychotherapy

Dorothea Huber & Guenther Klug

During the last few years, generally agreed-upon standards have been developed for the assessment of outcome in psychotherapy research. According to Lambert and Hill (1994, pp. 73–74), the state of the art requires:

1. assessment from different sources (self-reporting, trained observers, relevant others, therapist rating, institutional);

2. application of different, non-reactive technologies (global ratings, specific symptom index, observer ratings, physiological measures, life records);

3. atheoretic, pragmatic measures;

4. bi-directional measures;

5. multidimensional measures (intrapsychic, interpersonal, psychosocial);

6. follow-up measurements.

The rater training of the authors (DH and GK) with the PRP–II group in San Francisco at the California Pacific Medical Center was supported by the German Research Foundation DFG (444 USA 111/3/98). The inter-rater reliability and the validity study with the SPC are funded by a grant from the IPA.

Strupp, Horowitz, and Lambert (1997, pp. 30–32) developed the following criteria for a core battery to measure outcome:

1. clear and standardized procedures for administering and scoring the instrument;
2. norms for patient and non-patient populations;
3. demonstrated reliability;
4. demonstrated validity;
5. demonstrated sensitivity to change;
6. demonstrated feasibility in clinical settings;
7. systematic rater-training and calibration tapes available if administered by trained clinicians;
8. atheoretic measures;
9. multimodal measures;
10. categorical and dimensional measures;
11. measurement before, during, and after treatment.

Both approaches have to cope with the problem of grasping the mode-specific and therefore theory-bound effects of one specific therapeutic modality as well as applying theory-free, pragmatic measures not confined to the perspectives of one specific theory of change.

Schulte (1995, p. 285) tried to elucidate the dilemma by distinguishing four levels within the general concept of disease:

1. causes (biological, psychological, sociological);
2. disease (pathological changes in the person);
3. illness (symptoms, complaints, medical findings);
4. consequences (sick-role and impairment of normal role behaviour).

He argues that on Level 1, "causes", and Level 2, "disease", only school-specific and hence theory-bound measures are appropriate, while on Level 3, "illness", and Level 4, "consequences", theory-free measures are appropriate.

Reviewing the literature on the outcome of psychoanalysis and psychoanalytic psychotherapy, all authors (e.g. Roth & Fonagy,

1996; Vaughan, Marshall, MacKinnon, Vaughan, Mellman, & Roose, 2000) agree that, although some evidence of the effectiveness of these treatments has been accumulated, there still is a regrettable lack of studies that meet the requirements of modern empirical research.

One of their main points of critique has been the absence of appropriate measures to encompass the more ambitious aims of psychoanalysis and psychoanalytic psychotherapy. The outcome studies of the 1970s and 1980s mostly applied global assessments of therapeutic benefit that were not able to capture the specific effects of psychoanalysis and psychoanalytic psychotherapy. The outcome measures, largely expert ratings of interviews with the patient and the treating analyst, did not meet modern research standards such as, for example, reliability, validity, and sensitivity to change and could only cover dimensions of change in a very restricted way only, using vague categories. Bachrach, Galatzer-Levy, Skolnikoff, and Waldron (1991), therefore, concluded in their critical survey of outcome studies: ". . . the research methods, especially of the clinical-quantitative studies, reflect the state-of-the-art of the 1950s and 1960s more than currently available methods (p. 910)". Very much in the same vein is Luborsky, Diguer, Luborsky, Singer, Dickter, and Schmidt's (1993) critique of unsuitable outcome measures because they "do not make an adequate distinction between short-term and long-lasting improvement, nor do they make a distinction between the parallel related changes referred to as non-structural and structural change (p. 510)".

Another decisive point is that psychotherapy research shifted from the investigation of the outcome of psychotherapy to the connection between process and outcome. This brings about a new challenge for the conceptualization of outcome measures, because the link between outcome and process has to be observed attentively. As a principle that tries to meet the needs of process–outcome research, Strupp, Schacht, and Henry (1988) proposed the "Problem–Treatment–Outcome Congruence" (P–T–O Congruence method). Dahl (1988) elaborated on it thus:

> this principle [says] that the description and representation, theoretically and operationally, of a patient's conflicts, of the patient's treatment, and of the assessment of the outcome, must

be congruent, which is to say, must be represented in comparable, if not identical terms. [p. ix]

Therefore an outcome measure is needed that both grasps the
specific effects of psychoanalysis and psychoanalytic psychotherapy and is able to link the outcome, on a conceptual basis of a
commonly agreed-upon theory of change to the process, making
"psychoanalytic change" more conceivable that way.

Psychoanalysis and psychoanalytic psychotherapy used to understand Schulte's level (b) disease (pathological changes in the
person) as "psychic structure" and coined the term "structural
change" for changes on that level. Pulver (1991) defined psychic
structure "as any organisation of mental contents and processes
which, in a systematic way, carried out the various tasks of the
psyche". According to Piaget (1970) its basic principles are whole-
ness, transformation and self-regulation. The "Operationalized
Psychodynamic Diagnostics" group (OPD-Task Force, 2001) characterized "psychic structure" in terms of six features:

1. capacity for self-reflection;
2. capacity for self-management;
3. capacity for defence;
4. capacity for object perception;
5. capacity for communication;
6. capacity for binding.

Structural change as "the generally accepted goal of psychoanalysis" (Moore & Fine, 1990) and also to some degree of psychoanalytic psychotherapy (e.g. Kernberg, 1991; Wallerstein, 1986), is an
explanatory construct that tries to capture the specific effects of
psychoanalysis and psychoanalytic psychotherapy relating them to
the concept of psychic structure and their modifications by psychoanalytic treatment. Structural change signifies a type of change,
beyond symptoms and manifest behaviour, rooted in the matrix of
both. Kernberg (1991) defines it as a

> significant modification in the unconscious intrapsychic con-
> flicts underlying symptom formation. Change in the underly-
> ing unconscious intrapsychic structures is usually revealed in
> shifts in the equilibrium of ego, superego, and id, with a

significant expansion of the system ego and a corresponding
reduction of the pressures of the unconscious superego and id.
[p. 316]

The application of such global ego-psychological concepts in follow-up studies revealed, however, that they had to be more clearly
and differentially operationalized and had to be assessed by experts in order to grasp the more subtle effects of psychoanalytic
treatments (Wallerstein, 1986). As far as the technology (Lambert &
Hill, 1994) of the instrument and above all its non-reactivity are
concerned, we would like to point out that only expert clinicians
will be able to assess adequately the transference-related cognitive
distortions that regularly take place in follow-up interviews
(Pfeffer, 1959).

In summary, we conclude that an empirically founded outcome
measure that intends to grasp changes beyond symptoms and
behaviour in a process-outcome context, must:

1. be based on expert judgement;
2. be able to grasp different functions of psychic structure and
   their modifications;
3. be able to rule out the influence of symptoms on psychic
   functioning;
4. be able to assess the influence of transference-related cognitive
   distortions in the follow-up interviews;
5. be based on concepts agreed upon by adherents of different
   psychoanalytic schools;
6. have satisfactory psychometric qualities (reliability, validity,
   sensitivity to change, clinical significance);
7. must meet the requirements of the P–T–O principle.

We consider the Scales of Psychological Capacities (SPC)
(Wallerstein, 1991; Wallerstein, unpublished manuscript) as the
measure that best complies with these standards and that has
sufficiently proven its psychometric qualities (DeWitt, Hartley,
Rosenberg, Zilberg, & Wallerstein, 1991; DeWitt, Milbrath, &
Wallerstein, 1999).

Therefore we decided to apply the SPC to a comparative process–outcome study of psychoanalysis and psychoanalytic psycho-

therapies, the *Munich Psychotherapy Study* (MPS) (Huber & Klug, 1999; Huber, Klug, & von Rad, 1997, 2000), which is a process–outcome comparison study in progress that tries to answer two questions:

1. Are there any differences in effectiveness between psychoanalysis and psychodynamic psychotherapy? And if so, are those changes brought about by psychoanalysis based on "structural change", and as a result of this, are they more profound and more stable than those brought about by psychodynamic psychotherapy ?

2. Are there any links between therapeutic process and outcome? And, if so, what are they?

In order to answer the first research question, a randomized controlled design was chosen to compare the two experimental groups:

1. a group of patients treated with psychoanalysis (PA) taking place three times a week in a recumbent position with an average duration of 240–300 hours;

2. a group of patients treated with psychodynamic psychotherapy (PT) place once a week in a seated position with an average duration of 80–120 hours.

As already stated, the effectiveness of the two treatments can only be evaluated correctly if the patients are assigned at random to the two experimental groups. Because of the relatively small number of patients in each group ($n = 30$), a strict allocation at random would lead to an uneven distribution of important patient variables, which was one of the main issues of the NIMH (National Institutes of Mental Health) depression study (Elkin et al., 1989); we therefore decided to stratify the patients with regard to severity of symptoms and age. We set high value on the therapies being assigned at random and not the therapists, so as not to interfere with the important, individual patient–therapist match.

Each patient presenting at the outpatient department of the Institute of Psychosomatic Medicine, Psychotherapy and Medical Psychology of the Technical University of Munich who met the inclusion criteria received an extensive clinical intake interview that was audio-recorded. Based on this recorded interview, a board of three experienced psychoanalysts (the so called "indication board") decided whether the patient could be randomly assigned to one of the two experimental groups. This decision process was documented as precisely as possible.

The inclusion criteria were as follows: age between 25 and 45 years; ICD–10 diagnosis of depressive episode or recurrent depressive disorder; Beck Depression Inventory (BDI) (Beck, Ward, Mendelson, Mock, & Erbaugh, 1961) greater than 16; previous psychotherapy to have been finished at least two years before entering the study; not on anti-depressant medication; living in Munich or nearby; adequate German-language skills.

The ten therapists who participate in the study are experienced psychoanalysts and psychotherapists in private practice and have been working with patients for at least five years. They were trained at an approved institute and graduated from there. They only apply therapies in which they are experienced, and they are not obliged to apply a therapeutic modality they do not consider suitable for a particular patient.

The data come from three different sources of observation: the patient, the therapist, and the researcher ("external investigator"). The test battery of outcome measures is adapted from the core battery suggested by the Society for Psychotherapy Research (SPR), published by Grawe and Braun (1994), and chosen to be comparable with other ongoing studies.

As already stated, a major concern of the study is to measure not only symptoms and behaviour, but also mode-specific effects, and therefore special instruments to measure structural change and individual therapeutic goals are administered. Structural change is measured with the SPC; individual goals are assessed by means of the goal attainment scaling method developed by Kiresuk and Sherman in 1968, which in the Heidelberg Study of von Rad, Senf, and Bräutigam (1998) yielded an interesting discrimination between psychoanalysis and psychotherapy.

The procedural plan (schedule) of the study is shown in Table 4.1.

At the end of the intake interview with ICD–10 and DSM–IV diagnosis the external investigator completes the Global Assessment of Functioning Scale (GAF, DSM–IV, Axis V) (American

Table 4.1. Procedural Plan of the Munich Psychotherapy Study

Phase	Measurement
Pre-treatment	
external investigator 1 and patient	intake interview, ICD–10 and DSM–IV diagnosis, GAF, BADO, BDI (>16), BSS, HAMD
board of three experienced analysts	decision on patient's inclusion in the study
external investigator 1 and patient	SPC interview; informed consent
patient	self-rating questionnaires: BDI, SCL–90–R, IIP, FKBS, INTREX, SOZU, BADO, FLZ, FPI–R
external investigator 1 and patient	assessment of individual goals (goal attainment scaling, GAS); referral to therapist
therapist	documentation of diagnosis, psychodynamic hypothesis, level of personality organization, treatment goals, prognosis, HAQ–T
Process	Audio-recording of every session
patient	self-rating questionnaires: BDI, SCL–90–R, IIP, GAS and HAQ–P every 6 months
therapist	therapy accompanying card to be filled out after every session; periodical process-rating scale with HAQ–T every 6 months
Post-treatment	
external investigator 2 ("blind" for applied therapy) and patient	post-treatment interview, SPC interview, life-events checklist, ICD–10 and DSM–IV diagnosis, GAF, BSS, HAMD, BADO
patient	self-rating questionnaires: BDI, SCL–90–R, IIP, FKBS, INTREX, SOZU, BADO, FLZ, FPI–R, GAS, VEV, HAQ–P
therapist	periodical process-rating scale and HAQ–T, assessment of termination of treatment
Follow-up (annual)	
external investigator 2 and patient	follow-up interview, SPC-interview, life-events checklist, ICD–10 diagnosis, BSS, GAF, HAMD, BADO
patient	self-rating questionnaires: BDI, SCL–90–R, IIP, FKBS, INTREX, SOZU, BADO, FLZ, FPI–R, GAS, VEV

Psychiatric Association, 1994), the Symptom Severity Score (BSS) (Schepank, 1995), the Hamilton Rating Scale for Depression (HRSD) (Hamilton, 1960) and the Basic Documentation of the German College of Psychosomatic Medicine (BADO) (our version described by Huber, Henrich, & von Rad, 2000), including the rating of the psychic structure of the patient(Axis IV: Structure of the OPD) (OPD-Task Force, 2001). After a positive decision by the "indication board" and the obtaining of "informed consent" by the patient, the external investigator interviews the patient with a semi-structured SPC interview to obtain the appropriate information to score the SPC scales. In the third pre-treatment session the external investigator and the patient together assess the individual goals the patient wishes to achieve during the therapy. The patient is assigned to one of the experimental groups *after* this intake procedure, so that the external investigator is "blind" to therapeutic modality during the pre-treatment assessment.

Before the treatment starts, the patient completes the following self-rating questionnaires: SCL–90–R (Derogatis, Lipman, & Covi, 1975), Beck Depression Inventory (BDI) (Beck et al., 1961), Inventory of Interpersonal Problems, short version (IIP–C) (Horowitz et al., 1988), Introject questionnaire (INTREX) (Benjamin, 1974), Questionnaire for Coping Strategies (FKBS) (Hentschel, 1998), Freiburg Personality Inventory, revised version (FPI–R) (Fahrenberg, Selg, & Hampel, 1989), Life Satisfaction Questionnaire (FLZ) (Huber, Henrich, & Herschbach, 1988), Basic Documentation of the German College of Psychosomatic Medicine (BADO) (our version described by Huber, Henrich, & von Rad, 2000), Social Support Questionnaire, short version (F–SOZU–K–22) (Sommer & Fydrich, 1991).

The therapist completes the Helping Alliance Questionnaire (HAQ–T) (Alexander & Luborsky, 1986) and a documentation form with psychodynamic diagnoses, main defences, level of personality organization, motivation, main psychodynamic hypotheses, treatment goals, and prognosis. During the ongoing therapeutic process neither the patient nor the therapist is contacted personally, so as not to interfere with the process too much; of course, research itself inevitably influences the process. The process measures are sent to the patient and psychotherapist by post every six months. Each therapy session is audio-recorded.

Measurement points for the outcome measures are at pre-treatment, at post-treatment, and at follow-up each year after end of treatment. At post-treatment and follow-up the external investigator 2 is not the same person as at pre-treatment and is "blind" to the therapeutic modality—although the possibility of remaining "blind" during a clinical interview has been questioned in the literature (Luborsky et al., 1999). At post-treatment and follow-up the pre-treatment instruments are applied again, along with a retrospective life-event checklist and a self-rating questionnaire: Change in Experiencing and Behaviour, VEV (Zielke & Kopf-Mehnert, 1978).

The Scales of Psychological Capacities (SPC), the measure of mode-specific effects of psychoanalysis and psychoanalytic psychotherapy ("structural change") applied in our study, are an expert-rating measure that, while theoretically informed but not theory-specific, evaluates the level of psychic structure. They have been developed from the research methodology of the Psychotherapy Research Project (PRP) of the Menninger Foundation (Wallerstein, 1986) and try to operationalize the concepts of "psychic structure" and "structural change" as independently as possible of the differing theoretical perspectives in psychoanalysis, to enable them to assess reliably the specific changes after psychoanalyses and psychoanalytic psychotherapies. Bound to an empirical research strategy, these psychological capacities are designed to be as low-level (experience-near) constructs as possible and readily inferable from observable behaviours and conscious states of mind so that underlying intrapsychic structures and their changes after treatment can be reliably captured.

The SPC consist of 17 dimensions; 14 of these are, in turn, divided into 2 subdimensions, and 2 into 3 subdimensions; the remaining dimension is not divided. The assessment of all 36 subdimensions is based on a tape-recorded one-hour clinical intake interview, together with a one- to two-hour semi-structured SPC interview with probe questions, developed by the test author and his group. The material gained in this way is scored for each subdimension on a 7-point scale from 0, for "normal" or fully adaptive functioning, to 3, for functioning seriously and obviously disturbed, with half points in between. The dimensions are constructed such that one subdimension is designated for different degrees of inhibited functioning and another for different degrees of exaggerated functioning. Both directions have to be assessed, and both subdimensions can be scored simultaneously. The rating procedure requires an extensive manual with a detailed description of each subdimension, together with one or more clinical vignettes to anchor each scale point.

Although inter-rater reliability (DeWitt, Milbrath, & Wallerstein, 1999), content validity (DeWitt et al., 1991), and convergent validity (DeWitt, Milbrath, & Wallerstein, 1999) of the SPC have already been examined, there is a lack of studies that prove their feasibility for German research projects as well as a lack of discriminant validity studies.

Method

Any outcome measure needs to have sufficient evidence that reliability and validity are warranted as the basic psychometric properties. Developers of outcome measures must strike a balance between these two psychometric qualities to be able to offer instruments to researchers that meet their demands.

Comparing the SPC with instruments that measure interpersonal functioning and personality structure can evaluate convergent validity. Discriminant validity is evaluated in the present study by comparing the SPC with instruments measuring symptomatology.

We expect a zero or only a weak correlation between the SPC and the construct-distant measures and a moderate but not very high correlation between the SPC and the construct-near measures.

Validity Study I

As this pre-study has already been published (Huber & Klug, 1997; Huber, Klug, & von Rad, 2000), we provide only a short description of the procedure. The *sample* consisted of a homogeneous group of 41 depressed patients of the MPS study (see above). Two *judges* (DH & GK), both of them psychoanalysts with a completed analytic training and many years of professional experience, rated the 41 SPC interviews from the audiotapes. They trained themselves with the SPC manual and rated the first three interviews together. From then on they had recalibration sessions after every fifth rating. The construct-distant *instruments* were the SCL–90–R, a self-rating symptom inventory constructed to assess the psychological and symptom status of psychiatric patients on nine scales and a global severity index as well as on the BSS—an observer rating scale that evaluates the impact of psychic illness on three dimensions: physical, psychological, and social—and on the GAF (recent and highest level of functioning in the last year), which is an internationally used scale and is rated by the external investigator as well.

As a construct-near measure we used the Inventory of Interpersonal Problems—an internationally established instrument for assessment of interpersonal problems and concerns—in its self-rating form and, additionally, in an observer-rating form (Horowitz, personal communication) in order not to contaminate the results by changing the source of observation for the only measure used..

Inter-rater reliability study and Validity Study II

We performed a second construct validity study of the SPC as a replication of the above-presented convergent and discriminant validity studies to further examine validity three years later. This study consisted of another sample of the MPS, a different interviewer, different raters who were trained according to the formal method (Mercer & Loesch, 1979), and of additional construct-near and construct-distant instruments. As the validity of any diagnostic instrument presupposes a reasonable degree of inter-rater reliability, we started this time with an inter-rater reliability study. Neither study has yet been published; both are therefore presented in greater detail here.

Sample: Participants were a homogeneous group of 47 depressed patients, between the ages of 25 and 45 years. The diagnosis was made by an experienced clinician (psychiatrist and psychotherapist) using the International Diagnostic Checklist (IDCL) classification schema for ICD–10 and DSM–IV diagnosis (Hiller, Zaudig, & Mombour, 1995) after having discussed the cases with two other experts. According to the intake criteria, all patients had received a

Table 4.2. Description of the sample

Age: M = 34.6 years, *SD* = 6.5

Gender	female	66%
	male	34%
Marital status	single	66%
	married	19%
	divorced	15%
Romantic relationship		60%
Children		32%
Employment	full time	63%
	part time	11%
	unemployed	4%
	other	22%

diagnosis of a depressive disorder. A description of the socio-demographic data is given in Table 4.2 and the ICD–10 diagnosis in Table 4.3. The 38 patients in the inter-rater reliability study were a subsample of the above-described sample.

Procedure: The authors of this chapter attended a training course in the (Mercer & Loesch, 1979) formal method of rating with the PRP–II group in San Francisco; following this, they trained three

Table 4.3. ICD–10 Diagnoses

Diagnosis	Scale		%
First	F 32.1	depressive episode/moderate	43
	F 32.2	depressive episode/severe	17
	F 33.1	recurrent depressive disorder/moderate	23
	F 33.2	recurrent depressive disorder/severe	17
Second	F 34.1	dysthymia	47
		other	8
		no	45

German raters. After every fifth patient there was a recalibration session, where the three judges and the two trainers met to correct for judges' drift.

The two raters who came out with the best reliability scores rated the scales for Validity Study II. If they disagreed by more than one scale point, a senior rater (one of the authors) rated the scale again—a method recommended by Jones, Cumming, and Horowitz (1988).

Instruments: An instrument already used in the pre-study (Validity Study I) for construct-validity of the SPC, the IIP, short form (IIP–C) was used again. Additionally to the pre-study, we compared the SPC with the FKBS measuring five defence mechanisms/ coping strategies. A personality questionnaire (FPI–R) with 12 scales was added.

In addition to these self-rating questionnaires, the external investigator rates the psychic structure of the patient (OPD, Axis IV) on a 4-point scale ("good", "moderate", "low integrated", "disintegrated").

We again assessed discriminant validity with the SCL–90–R. Additionally, the Beck Depression Inventory (BDI) was used for assessment of the severity of depression.

Statistics: The inter-rater reliability between the three raters was calculated by means of Intra Class Correlation Coefficient (ICC) (Shrout & Fleiss, 1979) for all subdimensions separately.

Correlations between the SPC and the tests for discriminant and convergent validity were calculated with the Pearson Correlation Coefficient. Because of the large number of correlations computed, we decided to interpret only findings at a .1% level of significance.

Results

Validity Study I: At first content validity was examined by prospectively (i.e. before the respective subdimensions were scored on empirical material), assessing, from a clinical point of view, those subdimensions that would be expected to be most highly scored.

This clinically expected "prototypic" profile of depressive patients was compared with the empirically constructed profile. With only one exception, the empirically constructed mean profile of depressive patients was correctly predicted by the clinicians, very clearly demonstrating a high consensus between clinical judgement and SPC ratings.

The results of the discriminative and convergent construct validity study showed that there were no significant correlations between the SPC and symptoms measured by the SCL–90–R, the BSS and the GAF. There were 10 medium correlations ($rr = .49$ to .64) between the SPC and the IIP scales when IIP was rated by the patient (self-rating). There were 20 significant correlations between SPC and IIP scales when IIP was rated by the external investigator (judge rating). This can be readily understood, as it is well known that there is a higher correlation between data from the same source of observation than between the content of the scales. These results confirm the hypothesis that the SPC measure is relatively independent of current symptoms, and it measures something similar but not identical to interpersonal functioning (Huber, Klug, & von Rad, 2000).

Inter-rater reliability study: Because the judges could not discriminate reliably enough between the subdimensions "drudgery" and "apathy", these two subdimensions were condensed into one, which we called "apathy", thus reducing the number of subdimensions to 35.

The mean ICC was 0.82 within a range from 0.54 to 0.89. Using as a standard cut-off score a correlation level of .70, according to the recommendations of Lambert and Hill (1994) for scales that do not have a low level of inference, only 4 of the 35 subdimensions had reliabilities below this level. All of the 35 subdimensions reached Cohen's (1988) cut-off point of .50. These remarkable results for inter-rater reliability allowed the continuation of the psychometric investigation, and we conducted the extended validity replication study with a new sample, different interviewers, and different raters, as well as some additional instruments.

Validity Study II: Figure 4.1 shows the mean profile of our group of depressed patients on the 35 SPC subdimensions. This profile proves *construct validity* of the SPC because it operates in the expected way for depressed patients. The highest mean is for the subdimension "self-depreciation", followed by "overinvolvement in relationship", "internalization", "surrender of self", and "pessimism" (all means are above 1.5).

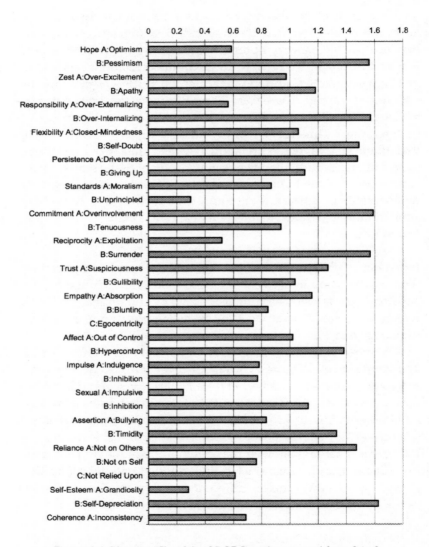

Figure 4.1 Mean profile of the 35 SPC scales, scored from 0 to 3.

Table 4.4. Significant correlations between subdimensions and instruments

	Scales	construct-distant	construct-near
SCL	10	0 (rr = .01 to .38)	
BDI	1	0 (rr = .02 to .41)	
BSS	4	0 (rr = .01 to .37)	
GAF	2	0 (rr = .01 to .32)	
FPI	12		12 (rr = .46 to .62)
IIP	9		16 (rr = .47 to .59)
FKBS	5		1 (rr = .52)
OPD	1		2 (rr = .48 to .49)

$p < .001$

Discriminant validity study: The data clearly show no significant correlations between either the SCL–90–R scales, the BDI, the Impairment-Severity Scores, or the two GAF scales and the SPC subdimensions plus the SPC total score (see Table 4.4).

Convergent validity study: As shown in Table 4.4, there are 12 significant correlations between the 12 FPI scales and the SPC (rr = .46 to .62, $p < 0.001$), and 16 correlations between the IIP scales and the SPC (rr = .47 to .59, $p < 0.001$). Of the five FKBS scales, there was only one significant correlation with the "turning against self" scale (rr = .52, $p < .001$); the other defence mechanisms did not correlate. The OPD rating correlated significantly with the SPC total score and the "coherence" subdimension (rr = .48 to .49, $p < .001$).

Conclusion

We consider the results of the inter-rater reliability study to be highly satisfactory, especially when taking into account that homogeneous samples tend to show considerably lower inter-rater reliabilities and that reliability is normally higher when instruments are applied by their developers (Zimmermann, 1994). Seen from an economic point of view, our reliability study suggests that raters do not need to have psychoanalytic training and are doing sufficiently well with medium-range rater training.

The results of the discriminant validity studies reveal clearly that there is no correlation between the SPC and the construct-distant measures, thus confirming our first assumption that the SPC measures beyond symptomatology.

The convergent validity studies with their considerable correlations between the SPC and the construct-near instruments offer convincing evidence that the SPC measures something similar, but not identical to interpersonal functioning and personality, thus confirming our second assumption.

We do not want to go into detail by interpreting single correlations, but nevertheless want to state that all inter-scale relationships were conceptually consistent and meaningful. We would like to point out that the significant correlation between the SPC and the "turning against self" scale of the FKBS can be interpreted as the "pathognomonic introjection" (Fenichel, 1945) of the depressive patient. This finding can be understood as another test of construct validity. The absence of any other correlations between the SPC and the remaining four scales of the FKBS suggests that the SPC does not measure just defence mechanisms, which is in accordance with our working model of "structural change" (Kernberg, 1991; Wallerstein, 1991).

We conclude from our psychometric studies that the SPC appears to be a reliable and valid instrument. The findings of Validity Study I were replicated in Validity Study II, although the interviewers and raters differed considerably in clinical experience, therapeutic education, and rater-training between Study I and Study II.

Although there is still much work to be done to establish other psychometric qualities—above all, sensitivity to change—there is already substantial evidence that researchers have available an instrument that measures psychic structure, which is a first step towards the measurement of structural change, the mode-specific effect of psychoanalysis and psychoanalytic psychotherapy.

CHAPTER FIVE

Close family or mere neighbours? Some empirical data on the differences between psychoanalysis and psychotherapy

Johan Grant & Rolf Sandell

A general background

Ever since Freud's time, there has been discussion about the differences and similarities between psychoanalysis and psychoanalytically oriented therapies. The questions discussed are theoretical, practical, and political in nature: Are the differences in indications, technique, and processes mainly a matter of *degree* or one of *quality*, the latter being a stricter distinction? Is it possible to develop a genuine psychoanalytic process in once- or twice-weekly treatment? Are psychoanalysts automatically qualified to do and teach psychotherapy? Should psychotherapy be taught as part of the psychoanalytic training?

The degree of segregation among the treatment modalities in the psychoanalytic part of the psychotherapy spectrum seems to vary between different countries. In Sweden psychoanalysts and

This chapter is an extended version of a paper presented at the Seventeenth World Congress of Psychotherapy, Warsaw, Poland, 23–28 August 1998.

psychoanalytically orientated therapists are quite careful—some would say meticulous—about the distinctions. (There has been a—sometimes heated—dispute between the two Swedish societies as to whether psychoanalysis could be conducted three times a week or whether this, by definition, should be called psychotherapy.) In Germany, on the other hand, the distinction is less clear, and the expanded term "intensive psychotherapy" (Dossmann, Kutter, Heinzel, & Wurmser, 1997) seems to be used to refer to a grey zone between psychoanalysis proper and low-frequency psychotherapy on a psychoanalytic footing. In this chapter we simply use the terms *therapy* and *therapist* as generic terms when we refer to the entire spectrum of psychoanalytic treatments and the terms *psychoanalysis* and *psychotherapy* when we refer specifically to psychoanalysis and psychoanalytically oriented psychotherapy.

In 1954 the American Psychoanalytic Association set up four full-day conference panels on the differences and similarities between psychoanalytically oriented psychotherapy and psychoanalysis proper. In the discussions two groups of participants emerged: those who viewed psychoanalysis and psychoanalytic psychotherapy as distinctively separate modalities (e.g., Bibring, 1954; Gill, 1954; Rangell, 1954) and those who would blur the boundaries or see none at all (e.g. Alexander, 1954; Fromm-Reichmann, 1954). Today, almost 50 years later, it seems as if the issues discussed and the groupings are pretty much the same, Kernberg (1999), for example, being in favour of clear distinctions and Fosshage (1997) favouring no clear distinction. (It is interesting to note that, with few exceptions, it is psychoanalysts who discuss these issues.)

From an empirical point of view there is indeed no evidence leading to a strict distinction between psychoanalysis and psychotherapy. To this day, the most ambitious project making a relevant comparison seems to be the Psychotherapy Research Project (PRP) of the Menninger Foundation, launched as early as in the 1950s. Based on the accumulated findings in the PRP, Wallerstein concluded clearly in favour of those who would blur the boundaries:

> The therapeutic modalities of psychoanalysis, expressive psychotherapy, and supportive psychotherapy hardly exist in ideal or pure form in the real World of actual practice. . . . [treatments] are intermingled blends of expressive-interpreta-

tive and supportive-stabilising elements . . . and . . . the overall outcomes achieved by more analytic and more supportive treatments converge more than our usual expectations for those differing modalities would portend; and the kinds of changes achieved in treatment from the two end of this spectrum are less different in nature and in permanence than is usually expected. [Wallerstein, 1989, p. 205]

Thus, contrary to what was to be expected, there were no differences in outcomes following psychotherapy and psychoanalysis; the mean effects of either treatment were quite modest; supportive techniques were as powerful as more interpretative ones; and psychoanalysts used supportive techniques to a greater extent than was usually assumed.

We believe that the findings of the Menninger study have been vitalizing to the discussion on the psychotherapy-versus-psychoanalysis issue by putting some empirical "facts" into focus. There is a need for more such empirical data. Unfortunately, there has been a strange lack of interest among psychoanalysts, psychotherapists, and, indeed, researchers in collecting systematic data on long-term psychoanalytic psychotherapy and psychoanalysis. Furthermore, the quality of the few systematic outcome studies that have been undertaken (as reviewed by Bachrach et al., 1991; Doidge, 1997; Kantrowitz, 1997) has generally been poor (Fisher & Greenberg, 1996). At the same time, research studies on process and outcome in short-term psychoanalytic treatment abound. Apart from making psychoanalysis and long-term psychotherapy vulnerable to attacks from adherents to so called empirically validated (usually short-term) treatments, the lack of empirical data has tended to transform important theoretical discussions into introvert academic hair-splitting, with little or no impact on training or practice. Humbly, we hope that the facts presented here will contribute to furthering the discussion.

In 1993 we launched the Stockholm Outcome of Psychotherapy and Psychoanalysis (STOPP) project. In this chapter we offer a condensed account of some of the results and, for the first time, present a questionnaire, The Therapeutic Attitudes Scale (TASC), which consists of three different scales, mapping what we like to think of as the *therapeutic milieu* that therapists provide for their patients. We have tried to avoid heavy technical and methodological descriptions and instead focus on results that we believe may challenge some of the conclusions drawn from the Menninger project.

Our approach is as follows. We begin with the background and the basic design of STOPP. Then we present data on patient characteristics and the general outcome. We introduce the Therapeutic Attitudes Scale (TASC) and some empirical differences between psychotherapists and psychoanalysts with respect to what they believe and what they do—or, at least, claim to do—in their offices. Finally, we present some data and a discussion on how the beliefs and attitudes of the treatment providers interact with treatment modality, producing differential effects in psychotherapy and in psychoanalysis.

Where we started: the study background

In 1989, the Swedish national health insurance authorities decided to specially fund projects to alleviate illnesses that were particularly burdensome to the national health insurance and health care systems. Among the various projects funded, one was for psychoanalysis and long-term psychotherapy with therapists in private practice. In Sweden, therapy is covered by the national health insurance system only as long as it is provided by a medical doctor. A majority of the licensed therapists, however, are not physicians. As many people do not have the ability, or are not prepared, to pay for long-term intensive treatment, we have, in effect, a situation with long waiting lists for therapy with medical doctors and an under-utilized capacity of therapy with non-physicians. The STOPP project was launched with grants from the national health insurance authorities. The main purpose was to study which people, under what circumstances, seek psychoanalysis or psychoanalytic psychotherapy. and what benefits they were able to derive from their treatments.

A programme supervisor decided on the subsidization of a treatment. To be eligible for a subsidy, the patient should first have contracted a licensed therapist and then have a written referral from another therapist, with a description of his or her need and suitability for the suggested treatment. The subsidy covered all costs up to three years, with no extensions allowed. (However, patients were free to continue treatment beyond the three years, financing it in other ways.) One—clearly unintended—effect of this rather bureaucratic procedure was that most patients' treatments had already started at the time of the referral. Also, we strongly suspect that in most cases the referring therapist made only a passive judgement of whether the person could benefit from the suggested treatment, rather than an independent assessment of what he or she believed was the treatment of choice for this particular patient. Hence, we believe that to a large extent we are dealing with "ordinary", usually highly motivated, patients who have actively chosen both their therapist and their mode of treatment.

What we did and why: the basic structure of the study

The project involved almost 1,200 patients in all. Our sample consisted initially of 756 persons: the 202 who had received subsidy between 1991 and 1993 and the first 554 on the waiting list for subsidy at the time of the first of three waves of follow-up, in 1994.

First, we read all the referrals in order to map what kind of patients we were dealing with. As it turned out that many patients were already in treatment at the time of the referral, assessment of pre-treatment status had to be based first and foremost on the referrals. To complicate matters further, diagnoses had to be made retrospectively for those who had already begun treatment: What had the case been when the patients started? Fortunately, most referrals described patients' histories in such a way as to make this possible. However, exact diagnoses could not be made with such a database, so each patient was only roughly diagnosed by a research assistant (psychologist) as having or not having a DSM–IV, Axis I or II diagnosis (American Psychiatric Association, 1994). We also assessed each person according to the GAF (DSM–IV, Axis V). In addition to the current state, based on the descriptions we also made a rating of the lowest level of functioning after age 18, which is an invention for this study. The reliability of our diagnostic efforts where checked with three judges making three independent diagnoses on a subsample of 20 patients. Despite the difficulties, the interrater reliabilities were found to be acceptable to very good: ICC = 0.69 for the presence of an Axis I diagnosis and 0.51 for the presence of an Axis II diagnosis, and 0.69 and 0.88 for current and lowest GAF, respectively.

Two postal questionnaires were the basic motors in our design: (1) the Well-being Questionnaire (WbQ), which was sent to all the patients in May 1994, 1995, and 1996, and (2) the Therapeutic Identity (ThId), which was sent to all treatment providers—that is, therapists and analysts—in the spring of 1996.

The WbQ is a 24-page booklet specifically designed for this project. It contained a series of questions and items focusing on demographic, familial, and socio-economic conditions; data on frequency and duration of ongoing or terminated treatment(s); previous treatments; sickness and health care utilization. It also included a number of well-known self-rating scales: the Symptom Checklist–90 (SCL–90) (Derogatis, Lipman, Rickels, Uhlenhuth, & Covi, 1974); the Sense of Coherence Scale (Antonovsky, 1987), and the Social Adjustment Scale (Weissman & Bothwell, 1976), all of which have high or very high reliabilities (between .60 and .90 in different studies). (These three scales were highly correlated—i.e. they either measured the same thing or were mutually dependent.) In this chapter we concentrate on the SCL–90 only. The SCL–90 consists of 90 items, each of which the patient is asked to rate, on a 5-point scale ranging from 0 (*not at all*) to 4 (*very much*), to what extent he or she has been troubled by various signs of somatic and psychic distress during the past seven days (for references on the reliability and validity of SCL–90, see Bridges & Goldberg, 1989).

After three reminders, about 60% of the sample had remained on the panel through all three waves. Here we present data from 331 persons who were or had been in long-term psychotherapy and 74 persons whose main treatment was, or had been, psychoanalysis (20 persons were excluded because of incomplete data; in addition, 12 highly unrepresentative persons who never started their treatments and 13 patients in various kinds of low-dose therapies, viz.

brief, low-frequency, group, or family therapies, were also excluded.) An analysis of the attrition revealed only small and typical differences between responders and non-responders. Those who did not want to partake in the study at all had lower current GAF before treatment, and those who dropped out of the study had lower levels of education and lower level of functioning according to current GAF ($ps < .05$; two-tailed t-tests and chi-squares). However, there were no differences in response rates among patients in psychotherapy versus psychoanalysis.

The ThId was distributed in 1996 to all 316 treatment providers (therapists and analysts) who had at least one patient (the range was 1 to 11 patients) in the project. For norming and standardizing purposes the ThId was also sent to a random sample of 325 Swedish therapists. The ThId consists of about 150 questions and/or items, divided into different sections. Apart from the TASC, which is described in detail below, there were three sections dealing with (1) basic education and professional training; (2) professional experience; and (3) personal therapy or training analysis.

It took four reminders to get 227, or 69%, of the national sample and 209, or 66%, of the 316 psychotherapists and psychoanalysts in the STOPP sample to complete the questionnaire. Chi-square analyses showed that attrition was not systematic (all $ps < .05$), except for the fact that therapists over 65 years of age in the national sample tended to abstain from responding on account of their retirement.

Who seek psychotherapy and who seek psychoanalysis?

Psychoanalytically orientated psychotherapists and psychoanalysts are sometimes accused of treating only "the worried well". There is a widespread notion that the typical patient in psychoanalytically oriented treatments is a "YAVIS" (young, attractive, verbal, intelligent, and social)—that is, well-off Woody-Allen-like characters whose main problem is an addiction to therapy. But when one reviews studies on consumers of psychotherapy and psychoanalysis, one will find that the typical patient bears only slight resemblance to this picture. In fact, she is an urban, middle-aged, well-educated, professional female, typically in a health-care, educational, or artistic profession (Carlsson, 1991, 1993; Garfield, 1994; Olfson & Pincus, 1994b; Vessey & Howard, 1993; Weber, Solomon, & Bachrach, 1985). At the same time, however, she is typically in a fairly bad shape in terms of her general medical condition, health-care consumption, and capacity to work. Indeed, this seems to be the case in Sweden (Carlsson, 1991, 1993; Schubert & Blomberg, 1994), as well as in the United States (Doidge, Simon, Gillies, & Ruskin, 1994; Olfson & Pincus, 1994a, 1994b) and in Germany (Dossmann et al., 1997).

In analysing the referrals we found that, in line with earlier findings, the patients in our sample appeared as a highly qualified group, educationally and vocationally. They were clearly not a representative sample of the general population, apparently rather belonging to the cream of the crop. However, based on the coarse pre-treatment diagnoses and some complementary pre-treatment data from the WbQ, we found that the patients were quite vulnerable and often highly distressed, with long self-reported histories of suffering and histories of psychiatric (mainly outpatient) care and use of psychoactive drugs. The typical patient had had psychiatric problems for more than five years, and the most frequent symptom was feelings of self-blame and stress for not having things done properly or on time (Items 26 and 86 on the SCL–90).

Table 5.1 shows the differences between patients in psychotherapy and psychoanalysis, respectively. Although they are similar in some respects, there were also some significant differences. As can be seen, there were relatively more men among the analysands. Analysands were also a few years older, had higher levels of education (which were already high among the psychotherapy patients), were more often married or divorced, and more of them had children. Psychiatrically, there were no, or only small, diagnostic differences or differences with respect to syndromes or level of disturbance according to the GAF scales. However, before the present treatment, psychotherapy patients tended to have utilized institutionalized psychiatry (inpatient or outpatient clinics, emergency rooms, etc.) to a larger extent, whereas analysands had, rather, turned to psychotherapy for help.

Table 5.1. Sociodemographic and diagnostic breakdown of psychotherapy patients and analysands

	Psychotherapy patients[a]		Analysands[b]		
	M	%	M	%	
Sociodemographic characteristics					
men		20		37	**
age	36		40		**
married and/or divorced		38		60	**
cohabiting with a partner		45		47	
has children		49		66	*
have some college education		76		94	**
DSM-IV categories					
psychiatric syndrome (Axis I)		58		54	
personality disorders (Axis II)		12		11	
no psychiatric diagnosis (v-codes)		33		36	
Level of functioning					
GAF, current	60		61		*
GAF, lowest after 18 years of age	52		54		
Previous psychiatric treatments					
any psychiatric treatment at all		79		91	*
psychotherapy		63		75	*
psychoactive drugs		55		56	
outpatient psychiatric care		56		45	
psychiatric emergency room		38		26	
hospitalized		21		10	*

[a]$n = 331$; [b]$n = 74$.
Note: * $p < .05$; ** $p < .01$, by *chi-square* and two-tailed *t*-tests for differences between the two modalities.

We conclude that, despite great similarities, there are some interesting differences between persons who seek psychotherapy and those who seek psychoanalysis. It seems that socio-economic and socio-cultural factors are the most important ones to distinguish between the two groups: the higher the social status, the more likely the patient is to be in psychoanalysis. One may only speculate on why this is the case. In general, highly educated people, especially in the social, educational, and health-care sectors or in the humanities, are familiar with, and take an active interest in, psychoanalytic thinking. They are, as Kadushin (1969) puts it, the "friends and supporters" of (psychoanalytic) therapy. The difference also mirrors the status or prestige differential between psychotherapists and psychoanalysts. Is it the patients or the therapists who generates it? Who chooses whom? Several studies suggest that the relationship between the social status of the psychotherapist and his or her patients indeed has to do with the fact that high-status therapists tend to choose high-status patients (Garfield, 1986; Kadushin, 1969; Lubin, Hornstra, Lewis, & Bechtel, 1973; Weber, Solomon & Bachrach, 1985). The social selectivity is, no doubt, a political problem, insofar as the treatment is paid for by public money. In Sweden the attacks on psychoanalysts and psychotherapists for their alleged lack of social concerns are frequent and, sometimes, harsh. Biological psychiatry and the cognitive–behavioural treatments maintain an attitude of being more attuned to "ordinary" or "lower-class" patients—by implication, those who "really suffer". As psychoanalysts and long-term psychotherapists lack empirical data, they tend to withdraw into a defensive position, sometimes claiming that the severe psychiatric patients are not really suitable for psychoanalytically orientated treatments. For one thing, this does indeed not seem to be the case, as far as our data show; for another, this offers an advantage to other kinds of treatments in the battle for public subsidy. The "worried-well" accusation does really not seem to be fair. Our interpretation is that it is the "burnt-out" and distressed professionals who seek therapy rather than bored housewives and artists looking for a pastime. A majority of them have tried different treatments, including drugs, before entering long-term treatment. Also, many had earlier tried other types of—usually less intensive—psychotherapy. A related question of great interest is whether retakes or new treatment are made less probable by long-term treatments? In fact, some of our findings suggest that this may, indeed, be the case (Blomberg, Sandell, Lazar, & Schubert, 1997).

Did patients get any better? The treatment effects

In order to answer this question, we had to partition our two treatment groups in such a way as to allow some form of comparison between subgroups before, during, and after treatment. As many of the patients had already started treatment by the time we started our project, because they had not waited for subsidy but started whenever they had found any way to finance it, we had no control over when patients in fact started or terminated treatment. Indeed, the timing of our follow-up questionnaire (the WbQ) was totally independent of where any one particular patient was in his or her treatment process. What we had, then, was a pool of patients in different phases of their treatment processes. Consequently, our first follow-up questionnaire "hit" the patient randomly with respect to where he or she was in the treatment process, before, during, or after treatment. Figure 5.1 is an attempt to illustrate this pictorially.

Consider three persons— Patients A, B, and C—with treatments extended in time, as indicated by the thick arrows. At the time of our first administration of the WbQ, Patient A had not yet begun her treatment, whereas Patient B was in treatment and Patient C had already finished hers. At the second administration (WbQ 2), Patient A had recently begun treatment, Patient B was a

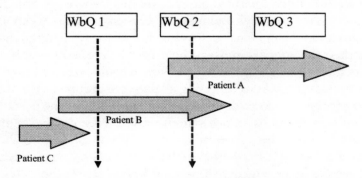

Figure 5.1. Examples of patients at different stages of treatment, in relation to waves of administration of the Well-being Questionnaire in 1994 (WbQ1), 1995 (WbQ2), and 1996 (WbQ3).

little bit further in hers, whereas Patient C was one year further post-treatment. By the time of the third administration (WbQ 3), Patient A was still in treatment, at a later stage in her treatment, whereas Patient B had now terminated treatment. Patient C was yet another year further in her post-treatment process.

The story of *Alice's Adventures in Wonderland* may be used as an analogy for how we designed our data-analyses. (This story is often used to illustrate another phenomenon in psychotherapy research: namely, the so-called Dodo-bird verdict, according to which "all [therapies] have won and all must have prizes".) At one point in the story, Alice had wept violently, creating a pool of tears crowded with birds and animals that had fallen into it. The Dodo then suggested a "Caucus-race" to get them dry:

> First it marked out a race-course, in a sort of circle (the exact shape doesn't matter, it said), and then all the party were placed along the course, here and there. There was no "one, two, three, and away", but they began running when they liked, and left off when they liked, so that it was not easy to know when the race was over. However, when they had been running half an hour or so, and were quite dry again, the Dodo suddenly called out "The race is over!" and they all crowded round it, panting, and asking "But who has won? [Carroll, 1865, pp. 32–33]

Using this analogy, in our "race", instead of the "race-is-over" call-out, we had three intermediate checkpoints (where we administered the WbQ), at one-year intervals. At each of these checkpoints we measured the patients' well-being (just as the Dodo might have measured the animals' pulse, if he'd been interested enough). At any of these checkpoints, any given patient could be before, during, or after treatment. After collecting all data, we grouped each of the 1,250 checkpoint scores or observations according to the point the patient's treatment had reached at the time: before, during, or after treatment and, more specifically, various subdivisions of each. In effect, we were able to position each checkpoint observation in one of seven phases on a relative time scale (Table 5.2). (Technically, we had a quasi-experimental design that is partly cross-sectional (across stages of treatment, across treatment modalities) and partly longitudinal (across successive stages of treatment).

Table 5.2. Number of observations at each of the seven treatments phases on a relative time scale

Phase	Observations
1. pre-treatment[b]	35
2. early treatment	186
3. mid treatment	207
4. late treatment	227
5. early post-treatment	232
6. mid post-treatment	207
7. late post-treatment	156

[a]n = 1,250; [b]in principle, we in fact had *three* phases before treatment: one with a number of observations on patients who never started any treatment at all and one with observations only on a small number of patients who were in kinds of treatments other than psychoanalysis or psychotherapy; these observations—and, accordingly, these phases—were therefore discarded.

In analysing the SCL–90 scores, we simply calculated and plotted the mean scores across all observations in each position along the 7-point time scale. Figure 5.2 shows a decay curve for each treatment group. (In technical terms, we created a partly within- and partly between-subjects design; we consider this equivalent to randomization, since our follow-ups were random with respect to patients' treatment processes—Chambless & Hollon, 1998.)

As can be seen, the analysands and psychotherapy patients started off at almost identical levels of symptom distress before treatment, and both groups then improved at about the same rate. However, after treatment termination the analysands continued progressively to improve, whereas the mean outcome flattened out asymptotically after psychotherapy. Analysing the linear trends, the intercepts and b *coefficients* were both significantly different from 0 in both groups [$t(6) = -8.07$, $p < .001$]. Also, the difference between the slopes in the two groups was significant [$t(12) = 4.08$, $p < .010$]. In terms of so-called effect size (d) the difference between the first and last values in the series was 0.59 for psychotherapy and 1.55 for psychoanalysis. According to research conventions, ds between 0.50 and 0.75 are moderate, and those over 1.00 are large.

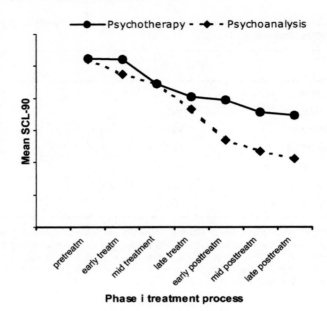

Figure 5.2. SCL–90 decay curves: mean SCL–90 scores for patients in psychotherapy and psychoanalysis across different phases of the treatment process.

Hence, the effect size for analysis is *very* large when compared to the effect sizes in the often-cited meta-analyses of, for example, Smith, Glass, and Miller (1980) and Shapiro and Shapiro (1982).

Now, how do we know that these differences do not stem from differences in patient characteristics? In fact, and as already noted, the patients were, indeed, not very different in absolute terms in the first place. However, to make sure, using regression-analyses, we partialled out diagnostic and demographic factors statistically and found that this did not change the differential trend.

More importantly: one might ask whether these differences were caused mainly by "extrinsic" factors such as treatment dose (Frequency × Duration), by the providers' formal competence, or mainly by "intrinsic" factors such as the therapeutic techniques used and the therapeutic processes that developed? There were, indeed, great differences with respect to the number of sessions in the two groups. The psychoanalyses had three to five sessions per week (M = 3.6, SD = 0.7) with a member of one of the psychoanalytic societies in Sweden (one within the International Psychoanalytical Association and one, at the time, within the International Federation of Psychoanalytic Societies; the psychotherapies were had one or two sessions a week (M = 1.5, SD = 0.5) with a psychotherapist licensed by the National Board of Health and Welfare. On average, then, the psychoanalyses had a total of 642 sessions (SD = 324) over about four and a half years (M = 54 months; SD = 23) and the psychotherapies 233 sessions (SD = 151) over nearly four years (M = 46 months; SD = 24).

The obvious question now is whether these extrinsic time factors, frequency, duration, and dose (the total number of sessions) account for the differences in effect that we observe. We have tried to sort this out in great detail using a sophisticated statistical procedure known as structural equation modelling (Jöreskog & Sörbom, 1986; Kline, 1998). It would be out of place to give a detailed account here. However, we found that the time factors *alone* could not explain the differences: neither frequency, nor duration, in and of themselves or separately, had any effect, whereas their interaction could explain *some* of the outcome variance (Sandell, Blomberg, & Lazar, 2002). Since patient variables could not explain the variance, we believe that other variables must be at work accounting for at least some of the differences. Next, we turn to one of these.

Different folks provide different strokes!
Differences and similarities among treatment providers

One important lesson from the Menninger project is that, in comparing psychotherapy and psychoanalysis, one cannot rely on any notion of a "standard" psychoanalytic or psychotherapeutic technique, since despite similar orientations and training, psychoanalysts and psychotherapists vary considerably in how they actually practice. Clearly, one main problem with our study was the lack of *direct* observations—through recordings or notes—of what had really been going on in treatment.

Of course, we might have tried to collect retrospective data from patients and therapists, but such retrospective data are indeed problematic, both from a methodological and from an ethical perspective. Our way of handling this was to develop a set of measures on therapist variables that we thought would be *related to* what might have been going on in the treatments. Of course, one cannot assume any one-to-one correspondence between words and deeds, and a therapist's technique will probably vary somewhat with the patient. However, it was—and is—our assumption that the therapist's beliefs and values in therapeutic matters help determine the general approach and technique he or she actually uses. Also, several studies indicate that therapists' intentions are in fact as strong, or even stronger, predictors of outcome than are their actual deeds (Hill, Helms, Tichenor, Spiegel, O'Grady, & Perry, 1988; Taylor, Adelman, & Kayser-Boyd, 1986). If we think of the consulting-room as a therapeutic "black box", one could say that we have not been able hear exactly what they are saying in it, but we can hear the tone of their voices.

The inventory we created is called the Therapeutic Attitudes Scale (TASC) and is part of the larger Therapeutic Identity questionnaire (ThId). The TASC consists of three sets of subscales: curative factors, therapeutic style, and basic assumptions:

1. The *curative factor* scales were based on 33 items, initially, to rate the therapist's beliefs in the curative value of each of a number of ingredients of therapy (e.g. helping the patient avoid anxiety-provoking situations). The instruction ran as follows: "What do you think contributes to long-term and stable therapeutic change?" The rating of each item was made on a five-step scale, from 0 (*not at all*) to 4 (*a lot*).

2. The *therapeutic style* scales were based on 31 original items to describe the therapist's own manner of conducting psychotherapy, in the general case ("What are you like as a therapist?"). Again, the items (e.g. I keep my personal opinions and circumstances completely outside the therapy) were rated on a 5-point scale, from 0 (*not at all*) to 4 (*a lot*).

3. The *basic assumptions* scales were based on an initial series of 16 items relating to one's more basic assumptions about the nature

of psychotherapy and the nature of the human mind, partly inspired by Hjelle and Ziegler (1981). The rating scales were continuous bipolar scales, with anchors at each of the poles offering a completion of the item stem (e.g. Psychotherapy may be described . . . as a science/as a form or art). The ratings were later transformed to 5-point scales. To encourage wider use of the scales, the scales and their items are presented in the Appendix.

When we analysed the TASC-scales, we found several important and significant differences within the sample. Figure 5.3 shows the relative difference between the treatment providers. As can be seen, patients in psychotherapy—which were, indeed, sometimes conducted by people with psychoanalytic training—were treated in a therapeutic milieu that was more similar to what we had found characteristic of behavioural and cognitive therapists in the national sample. The psychotherapy providers did put significantly

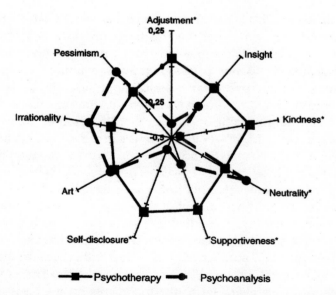

Figure 5.3. Mean z-scores on the TASC for treatment providers in psychoanalysis (broken line) and in psychotherapy (unbroken line); curative factors: "adjustment", "kindness", "insight"; therapeutic style: "supportiveness", "self-disclosure", "neutrality"; basic assumptions: "art", "irrationality", "pessimism".

greater value than the psychoanalysis providers on promoting *adjustment* and showing *kindness* as curative factors ($ds > 0.43$, $ps < .05$). Psychotherapy providers also preferred a technique that was less *neutral* and higher on *supportiveness* and *self-disclosure* ($ds > 0.26$; $ps < .05$) than the psychoanalysis providers. However, there were no significant differences with respect to the basic assumptions, although those providing psychoanalysis were a little bit higher on *pessimism* and *irrationality* ($ds > 0.23$; n.s.).

Based on the scores on all nine sub-scales (using cluster analyses), each therapist was then assigned to one of the four standard clusters, based on the national sample (described in the Appendix). The distribution was as follows:

- 42% were assigned to psychoanalytic cluster
- 34% and 24%, respectively, were assigned to the eclectic clusters
- 0% were assigned to the cognitive/cognitive–behavioural cluster

Thus, if we are to believe that treatment is carried out in rough correspondence with what the treatment provider believes and values—or at least claims to believe and value—we find that neither psychoanalysis nor psychotherapy is a unique or specific designation of any particular technical approach. The division of the therapists into three—or at least two—distinct clusters is all the more interesting in light of the fact that, in response to a direct question in the ThId, 95% of the therapists in our sample claimed to endorse a "psychoanalytic orientation". That psychoanalytically orientated psychotherapists as well as psychoanalysts hold insight in high esteem and value neutrality as a technical attitude is, of course, not astounding—although the value of neutrality may not be as great, generally, in conducting psychotherapy as in psychoanalysis. Over and above sharing these basic tenets, however, therapists will vary in a number of other respects that we assume will make an essential difference in the treatment office. This is news, we believe. If we characterize the treatments on the basis of the therapist's cluster membership, there was a minority (30%) of eclectically orientated psychoanalyses (and hence 70% were classically psychoanalytic). Among the psychotherapies, there was a more even distribution of treatments conducted in an orthodox psychoanalytic vein (43%), or in a more eclectic way (57%), with attitudes more characteristic of cognitive and cognitive–behavioural therapies.

Thus, what we have found quite frequently among so-called psychoanalytically orientated psychotherapists, and not infrequently among psychoanalysts, is a particular constellation of attitudes that we would consider a more sociable, if not humane, attitude in relating to the patient, which is partly at odds with the neutral attitude or with a generally psychoanalytic attitude. In conjunction with the positive valuation of insight and neutrality, these attitudes reflect what we have chosen to call an eclectic type of approach, which, we would hypothesize, is more closely connected to what is usually described as the aims of psychoanalytic psychotherapy than those of psychoanalysis proper.

The relationship between
therapeutic milieu and outcome

Now, the obvious question is: "Which type of therapist did best?" Although this question may seem simplistic, few therapists would doubt that the personal and professional qualities are of great importance in contributing to good or not-so-good treatment results. Also, most training institutes put heavy emphasis on "suitability" for becoming a therapist. However, there is little or no empirical support for any given characteristic, even though therapist expectations and qualities are among the most frequently studied variables in outcome research. In summarizing this research, Beutler, Machado, and Neufeldt (1994) draw three conclusions: (1) Individual therapist variables account for more variance in outcome than does mode of therapy. (2) Some therapists are better than others. (3) Some therapists are detrimental to clients. However, apart from this, the relationships between outcome and therapist variables are highly unclear: There is little or no consensus as to which traits of therapists are predictive of outcome. And, according to the well-known Dodo bird verdict, theoretical orientation *per se*—in terms of the usual coarse distinctions we make, psychodynamic, cognitive, or behavioural—are obviously not predictive of outcome.

In order to study the relationship between therapists' values and patient outcome, we paired all patients with their respective therapists. We then had data from 330 therapist–patient couples, 55 in psychoanalysis and 275 in long-term psychotherapy.

When the three clusters were compared on the basis of outcomes among their patients, we found that, in general, therapists providing an orthodox psychoanalytic milieu had significantly *worse* results than did those providing a more eclectic milieu did. Also, when we compared therapists high (above the median) on single TASC scales with therapists low (below the median) on the scales, we found significant differences in favour of attitudes on which the members of the psychoanalytic cluster were rated low. Thus, the strongest associations with good outcome were found with therapists high on "kindness" and "supportiveness", neither of which were favoured by the orthodox attitude; "art", favoured by neither the orthodox nor the eclectic attitude; and "neutrality", favoured by the orthodox view (all *ps* < .05). Clearly, these findings came as a surprise, since they were rather at odds with the fact that patients treated in psychoanalysis did better. How could this be? The riddle got its answer when we distinguished between the psychotherapy and the psychoanalysis cases and assigned the cases of each type to one of the two main groups: those who had been offered an eclectic milieu and those treated in an orthodox psychoanalytic milieu. The former group was made up of those cases where treatment was provided by therapists in any of the two eclectic clusters and the latter of cases treated by therapists in the orthodox analytic cluster. Figure 5.4 shows the results.

Obviously, for patients treated in psychotherapy, the two types of therapists did significantly differently. Psychotherapy provided in an orthodox psychoanalytic milieu had significantly worse outcomes than did psychotherapy in an eclectic milieu. In fact, the mean change among the former cases did not differ significantly from 0 [$b = -0.007$, $t(6) = 0.33$, n.s.],versus that [$b = -0.101$, $p = .000$] for the eclectic group. Among the psychoanalysis cases there was, indeed, a difference in the same direction, but one that was not at all significant [$b = -0.140$, $p = .006$ versus $b = -0.087$, $p = .012$]. Thus,

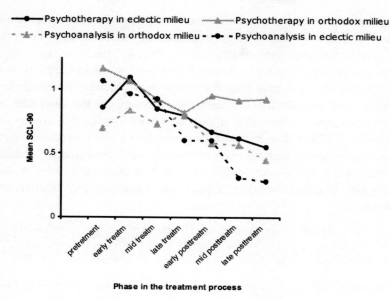

Figure 5.4. SCL–90: Decay curves for patients treated in an orthodox psychoanalytic milieu or in an eclectic milieu: mean SCL–90 scores for patients in psychotherapy (unbroken lines) and psychoanalysis (broken lines).

what seems to make a *large* difference in psychotherapy does not seem to (as much) in psychoanalysis.

Closing comments

There currently seems to be a trend towards a blurring of the boundaries between psychoanalytic psychotherapy and psychoanalysis proper. The lack of data supporting a clear distinction, the multiplicity of psychoanalytic theories, and the pluralism and relativistic trend within psychoanalysis (Fosshage, 1997) all work in this direction.

Although there are, indeed, great similarities between the two, our results indicate that there are also some very important differences between psychoanalytic psychotherapy and psychoanalysis in patients, outcome, therapist attitudes, and techniques. The most interesting finding, however, is that a strict psychoanalytic attitude does not seem to be really appropriate in psychotherapy. The "as-if psychoanalyses" are clearly not successful. This is, we believe, a very important finding that may justify the theoretical discussions.

However, it seems that the theoretical discussions on differences and similarities are very often based on the—explicit or implicit—assumption that a psychoanalytic process is always a good one. Often it seems that the proponents of a clear distinction as well as those against such a division end up drawing similar conclusions. For example, Gill (1988), a "separatist", closes a discussion on the conversion of psychotherapy into psychoanalysis, thus:

> The question of converting psychotherapy into psychoanalysis should rarely arise in the practice of a psychoanalyst because almost always he should be practising psychoanalysis. [p. 262]

Fosshage (1991), from the other position, ends up concluding that

> What's critical is not the differentiation between psychoanalytic psychotherapy and psychoanalysis, but the consistent application of expanded psychoanalytic technique within the work that we do as psychoanalysts. . . . In this sense, psychoanalytic psychotherapy cannot be substituted for (or, I will add, converted into) psychoanalysis, it *is* psychoanalysis. [pp. 70–71]

No matter the starting point or line of argument, then, there seems to be a norm where "the more psychoanalytic the better"!

Our results challenge such a view. Gill (1954, 1984) has suggested two definitions of psychoanalysis, the "intrinsic criteria" being analysis of transference, a neutral analyst, the induction of a regressive transference neurosis, and the resolution of that neurosis by interpretation, whereas the extrinsic criteria are "frequent sessions, the couch, a relatively well integrated (analysable) patient . . . and a fully trained psychoanalyst". Indeed, there have been many articles dealing with the question of whether a psychoanalytic process (the intrinsic criteria) can take place when extrinsic criteria are not met. However, we want to approach the question from a slightly different point of view.

Assuming a relationship between what we have called "the therapeutic milieu" and Gills' intrinsic criteria, the interaction between therapeutic milieu and treatment modality could be interpreted to mean that an orthodox psychoanalytic attitude is, indeed, sub-optimal or even dysfunctional in a setting that is not psychoanalytic. Put another way: both the intrinsic and the extrinsic criteria should be met in order for psychoanalysis to be successful. It may be that a psychoanalytic process, as fostered by an orthodox neutral, interpretative, and transference-focused stance of the analyst, may become destructive, mystifying, or confusing to the patient when the extrinsic criteria are not met. The primary question, then, is not whether a genuine psychoanalytic process *can* take place when extrinsic criteria are not met but, rather, whether it is good that it does.

We suggest that, instead of thinking of psychoanalytic psychotherapy as a diluted, or second-rate, form of psychoanalysis, it is more productive to think of it as a unique way of treating patients. Even if it relies on the psychoanalytic theories about pathogenesis and about psychic life in general, psychoanalytic psychotherapy may find its future in openness to other bases of knowledge *as well* as the psychoanalytic where therapeutic technique is concerned. This does not necessarily mean that psychoanalytically oriented psychotherapists—or, for that matter, psychoanalysts doing therapy—should adopt whatever is in fashion; rather, it means that they should develop an openness to the multiplicity of therapeutic schools currently at hand. We agree with Kernberg's (1999) view that an active experimentation with different techniques paired with critical systematic research is the best basis for providing fruitful technical advances in both psychoanalytic psychotherapy and psychoanalysis proper.

This leads to the question of whether psychoanalysts are automatically qualified to do and teach psychotherapy. Our answer would be that there are good reasons for psychoanalytic institutes to teach psychotherapy to their candidates. Many psychoanalysts have a hard time nowadays trying to earn a living by doing psychoanalysis only, and therefore they do psychotherapy instead. It is important that they realize that they should in that case not engage in some kind of diluted, "as-if" psychoanalysis. Also, in Sweden, psychoanalytically oriented therapists are usually trained and supervised by psychoanalysts. Based on our findings, the sometimes elevated status of psychoanalysts in Swedish training institutes for psychotherapists could be questioned. Again, we agree with Kernberg (1999): a clear delimitation between psychoanalysis and psychoanalytic psychotherapy could help provide a good basis for broadening and deepening the understanding of curative factors and the different pathways to therapeutic change. We conclude that courses in psychotherapy within the analytic institutes could both enrich the analysts' educational experience and contribute to a mutually productive exchange between psychotherapists and psychoanalysts.

APPENDIX

Standardization of the Therapist Attitude Scales (TASC)

For standardization purposes, the items in the TASC subscales were factor analysed, using data from the national random sample of licensed therapists. In an exploratory series of analyses, using various extraction and rotation methods and various principles for determining the number of factors, we found a stable and interpretable solution for each of the three item sets when three factors were extracted and rotated for each section. The highest-loading items in each such factor were subsequently used for forming factor scales. Thus, for each of the three first components in each set, a score was computed as the mean across all high-loading items (after transforming scores on items in the section on basic assumptions to a 5-point scale, as for the other scales). As high-loading items we considered those that had routinely turned up with loading higher than, or around, .5 in the exploratory series of analyses. For items in the "basic assumptions" section our criterion had to be set a bit lower, at .4, in order to have enough items left. The items constituting each of the nine scales are listed in Table 5.3.

As a validation of the scales, we tested whether they differentiated as expected between therapists with different theoretical orientations and with different schools of training as the basis for their licensing. The results of these tests are exhibited in Figure 5.5 (top and middle panels). For reasons of readability, the relatively small groups of therapists with family or group training were

Table 5.3. The Therapeutic Attitudes Scales

- **Curative factors ("What do you think contributes to long-term and stable therapeutic change?")**

Promoting adjustment ("Adjustment")

1. Giving the patient concrete goals
2. Working for adjustment to prevailing social circumstances
3. Helping P avoid anxiety-provoking situations
4. T takes the initiative and is leading the sessions
5. Stimulating P to think about his problems in more positive ways
6. Working with P's symptoms
7. Giving P concrete advice
8. Helping P control his/her feelings
9. Helping P avoid repeating his/her mistakes

Promoting insight ("Insight")

10. Helping P understand that old reactions and relations are repeated with T
11. Helping P see the connections between his/her problems and his/her childhood
12. Supporting P to ponder, in the therapy, painful early experiences
13. Working with P's defences
14. Bringing P's sexuality to the fore
15. P has the opportunity to work with his/her dreams
16. Help P understand that old behaviours and relations are being repeated
17. Interpret P's body language
18. Working with P's childhood memories

Showing kindness ("Kindness ")

19. The therapist is warm and kind
20. The patient feels well liked by the therapist
21. Supporting and encouraging the patient
22. Consideration and good care-taking
23. Let the patient get things off his chest

- **Therapeutic style factors ("What are you like as a therapist?")**

Neutral attitude ("Neutrality")

1. I do not answer personal questions from the patient
2. I keep my personal opinions and circumstances completely outside the therapy
3. I am more neutral than personal in therapy
4. I do not express my own feelings in the sessions
5. My verbal intervention are brief and concise
6. Keeping the therapeutic frame is an important instrument in my work

Supportive attitude ("Supportiveness")

7. I often put questions to the patient
8. It is important to convey hope
9. It is important to order and structure the material
10. I am rather active in sessions

(continued)

Table 5.3. The Therapeutic Attitudes Scale (*continued*)

Self-disclosing attitude ("Self-disclosure")

11. I always communicate the therapeutic goals to the patient in the beginning of a therapy
12. I always make the therapeutic goals explicit to myself during a therapy
13. I admit my own mistakes to the patient

- **Basic assumptions ("What are your general beliefs about the human mind and about psychotherapy?")**

Rationality v. irrationality ("Irrationality")

1. Human behavior is governed . . . by free will/by uncontrollable factors
2. By nature, man is . . . rational/irrational
3. Human behavior is governed . . . by external, objective factors/internal, subjective factors

Craft v. Art ("Art")

4. Psychotherapy may be described . . . as a craft/as free creative work
5. Therapeutic work is governed . . . by training/by personality
6. Psychotherapy may be described . . . as a science/as a form or art
7. Psychotherapeutic work is governed by . . . systematic thinking/intuition

Optimism v. pessimism ("Pessimism")

8. The basic principles of human behavior may be understood . . . completely/not at all
9. Humans can develop . . . infinitely/not at all
10. Therapeutic work is governed by the fact . . . that everything may be understood/ that not everything may be understood

---

excluded from Figure 5.5 (middle panel). As will be seen, neither "irrationality" nor "pessimism" had any significant relation with theoretical orientation, as rated by the therapists themselves. They were also less strongly associated with training varieties. Furthermore, "kindness" discriminated less well among groups with different theoretical orientations (Figure 5.5, top panel). Otherwise, however, the TASC was strongly discriminative in a pattern that is wholly consistent with theoretical suppositions.

In order to study the variation among the treatment providers further, we then performed a series of cluster analyses. As before, we used the national random sample of therapists and applied Anderberg's (1973) "nearest neighbour" method as a suitable technique with large samples. After an exploratory series of analyses, we finally settled for a four-cluster solution, which meaningfully

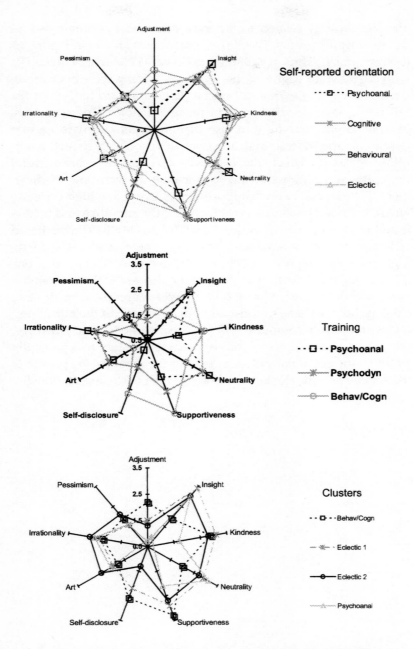

Figure 5.5. Relationship between TASC scores and self-reported theoretical orientation (top panel), type of training (middle panel), and cluster (bottom panel).

and significantly related to different theoretical orientations and different training sites. The cluster profiles are shown in Figure 5.5 (bottom panel). Thus, we found one cluster (12%) where therapists with cognitive or cognitive–behavioural training were over-represented; one (27%) with a rather complementary profile across the self-rating factors, with an over-representation of persons with psychoanalytic training (but also including persons with regular psychotherapeutic training); and two with profiles high on the self-rating scales on which the cognitive and cognitive–behavioural therapists were high and the psychoanalysts were low ("adjustment", "kindness", and "supportiveness") and *also* high on those where the psychoanalysts were high and the cognitive and behavioural ones were low ("insight" and "neutrality"). They differed radically on "self-disclosure", however, one cluster (34%) being high (like the cognitive/cognitive–behavioural cluster) and one (27%) being low (like the psychoanalytic cluster). Different training sites, with local particularities, were over-represented in the two clusters, but we chose to consider both as eclectic in their attitudes, endorsing *both* behavioural and psychoanalytic values. However, the profile of the larger of the two eclectic clusters was generally closer to the cognitive–behavioural cluster, whereas the profile of the smaller eclectic cluster was closer to the psychoanalytic cluster.

CHAPTER SIX

Psychoanalytically orientated day-hospital treatment for borderline personality disorder: theory, problems, and practice

Anthony W. Bateman

In this chapter I discuss some general problems of research into personality disorder (PD), outline some of the difficulties faced in organizing research into borderline personality disorder (BPD), and, finally, summarize the results of the first randomized controlled trial of outcome of treatment of BPD in Britain (Bateman & Fonagy, 1999, 2001).

BPD is common, affecting about 1% of the general population and up to 20% of psychiatric inpatients. Approximately 9% of BPD patients eventually kill themselves (Frances, Fyer, & Clarkin, 1986). This fact alone means that finding effective treatment is urgent, and yet, despite over two decades of research, our knowledge of the disorder and its treatment remains limited. The complexity of the disorder, characterized by "stable instability", baffles clinicians and researchers alike. Characteristics of impulsivity, self-destructiveness, constant efforts to avoid real or imagined abandonment, chronic dysphoria, sudden anger or boredom, transient psychotic episodes or cognitive distortions, and identity disturbance all militate against a smooth ride for researchers and clinicians. It is therefore not surprising that many continue to avoid borderline patients, finding them frustrating and impossible. Despite these problems, our unit set out to investigate a psychoanalytically orientated treatment for BPD using a randomized controlled design. It soon became apparent why there has been only one other randomized controlled trial (RCT) of BPD (Linehan et al., 1991)!

Problems of outcome research into personality disorder

There are few controlled trials of treatment for BPD. There are a number of reasons for this. (1) There are problems of case identification and co-morbidity. Although enshrined in diagnostic classifications, concern about the validity of the diagnosis remains. An overlap with affective disorders exists, but Gunderson and Phillips (1991) have concluded that the two disorders are not the same, although affective instability is at the heart of BPD. (2) BPD is an heterogeneous condition and varies in severity. Until recently there was no measure of severity, making it impossible to assess the level of morbidity in a sample of patients. Crude attempts to establish severity at the outset of treatment or entry into a trial such as counting acts of self-harm over the preceding weeks or months probably bear little, if any, relationship to severity. A patient who makes serious suicide attempts at infrequent intervals may be more seriously disturbed than is a patient who frequently, albeit usually sporadically, takes overdoses. (3) Finally, there is the difficulty of random assignment, which has now become the gold standard against which treatments are tested.

Randomization

Borderline patients do not take kindly to randomization. Their search is for stability and certainty. Offering them referral into a research project in which their allocation appears to be dependent on the toss of a coin confronts them with uncertainty and makes them vulnerable to fears of rejection. Both randomization in and randomization out cause problems. Borderline patients at the severe end of the spectrum have usually had years of psychiatric treatment and psychotherapy. Each new offer of treatment is a moment of hope. For those accepted into treatment, early expectations may not be met. When confronted with the reality of hard therapeutic work, the result may be, at best, a feeling of demoralization and, at worst, rage and aggression and refusal to participate in any further aspect of research. Randomization out of the treatment into a control group can lead to refusal to co-operate. Yet the researcher needs patients who are randomized out of the treatment programme to agree to further interviews and to fill out questionnaires. This can become progressively more difficult over time, leading to a high attrition rate in a control group, distorting the cohort of patients. Some patients may even take pleasure in ensuring that researchers do not get the information they ask for at the time that it is needed, leading to further sampling problems. Given the relatively small cell sizes of RCTs, attrition represents a serious threat to internal validity. PD patients tend to show relatively high attrition rates in treatment trials (Tyrer et al., 1990) although this varies according to personality disorder diagnosis (Shea et al., 1990) and treatment approach (Bateman & Fonagy, 1999; Linehan et al., 1991; Rosser et al., 1987).

In addition to the sampling problems discussed above, there are other difficulties. (1) There is an accumulating literature on the importance of patient expectations for therapy outcome (Horowitz, Rosenberg, & Bartholomew, 1993). Strict randomization may lead to treatment allocations incongruent with patient expectations, and this may be particularly problematic for patients whose lack of flexibility is almost a defining feature of their disorder (Bleiberg, 1994). (2) RCTs, with notable exceptions (Shapiro et al., 1995), do not randomize therapists to patients, even though it is known that the personality, skills, and training of the therapist have significant effects on outcome (Beutler, Machado, & Neufeldt, 1994). This potential confound is likely to be even greater for psychotherapeutic treatments of PD, given that interpersonal relationship problems are undoubtedly at the core of personality disturbance. (3) Investigator allegiance (Robinson, Berman, & Neimeyer, 1990) has been shown to strongly affect outcome, and unbiased, blind evaluations are hard to achieve in long-term treatments. (4) Comparison groups are difficult to identify for long-term therapy trials. A no-treatment comparison is ethically unacceptable in BPD (Basham,

1986), particularly as suicidality and self-harming behaviour are common. On the other hand, as long-term therapy tends not to be routinely available, a treatment-as-usual control group may be valid and appropriate.

There is a trade-off between the internal validity (Cooke & Campbell, 1979) of well-controlled trials, which ensure that causal inferences may be appropriately drawn from experimental manipulations, and the external validity of naturalistic research designs, which are limited in terms of causal inference but generate findings more readily generalizable to everyday practice (Hoagwood, Hibbs, Brent, & Jensen, 1995; Jensen, Hibbs, & Pilkonis, 1996). At the extreme end of naturalistic studies are survey reports, such as the consumer survey of psychotherapy (Seligman, 1995). Of course, what is sacrificed in surveys is information about the exact nature of the treatment offered and information from individuals who did not respond. Imposing strict controls, however, carries a cost in depicting psychotherapy in a far more organized and coherent form than is available in the real world of the clinic. No wonder, then, that clinic-based studies tend to regularly under-perform more strictly performed laboratory-based investigations (Weisz, Donenberg, Han, & Weiss, 1995).

But, most importantly, the absence of a clear distinction between even manualized treatment interventions has contributed to the lack of progress on specifying particular therapeutic approaches to BPD. Outcome evaluation is hampered by the lack of specificity in psychological approaches to therapy (Roth, Fonagy, & Parry, 1996), and some have argued that the considerable overlap between psychotherapies compromises the possibility of reaching conclusions concerning relative effectiveness (Goldfried, 1995). The problem is, once again, particularly acute in the case of the long-term approaches used in treating personality disorder. With such patients, practitioners make complex choices in selecting interventions that take account of both behavioural and dynamic factors. In order to enhance specificity, researchers have "manualized" treatments and developed measures to assess the extent to which therapists are able to follow protocols outlined therein. Three approaches to therapy with BPD—psychoanalytic psychotherapy (Clarkin, Kernberg, & Yeomans, 1999), dialectical behaviour therapy (DBT) (Linehan, 1993b), and object relations/interpersonal approaches

(Dawson, 1988; Marziali, Newman, Munroe-Blum, & Dawson, 1989)—have been manualized so far. The manual for cognitive–analytic therapy is as yet untested (Ryle, 1997).

Treatment intervention

The modified individual psychoanalytic approach adopted by Kernberg (Clarkin, Kernberg, & Yeomans, 1999) is based on clarification, confrontation, and interpretation within a developing transference relationship between patient and therapist. Initially there is a focus and clarification of self-destructive behaviours both within and outside therapy sessions. Gradually aspects of the self that are split off from the patient's core identity are challenged, especially as they impinge on chaotic impulsive behaviour, fluctuating affects, and identity conflict, which itself leads to dissociation. Understanding and resolving their impact on the transference relationship becomes central. Considerable work on elaborating and validating this therapeutic approach has been performed as part of an NIMH-funded treatment development project, demonstrating that it is possible to train clinicians to use this method (Clarkin et al., 2001).

In contrast, Linehan's strategy in DBT uses support, social skills, education, contingency management, and alternative problem-solving strategies to manage impulsive behaviour and affect dysregulation. A mix of both individual and group psychotherapy is used. However, the relationship between patient and therapist is pivotal in helping the patient to replace maladaptive actions such as self-destructive acts with adaptive responses during crises. Linehan (1993a) suggests that a number of aspects "set if off from 'usual' cognitive and behavioural therapy" (p. 20) and that "the emphasis in DBT on therapy-interfering behaviours is more similar to the psychodynamic emphasis on 'transference' behaviours than it is to any aspect of standard cognitive–behavioural therapies" (p. 21).

The treatment strategy developed by Dawson (1988) and colleagues is named "Relationship Management Psychotherapy" (RMP). In essence, this approach conceptualizes the borderline patient as struggling with conflicting aspects of the self, leading to instability. Interpersonal relationships, including the therapeutic relationship, become the context in which the patient tries to resolve conflicts through externalization. For example, if a therapist is optimistic and active, the patient becomes pessimistic and compliant. In some ways such polarities are similar to the reciprocal roles identified in cognitive analytic therapy. The role of the therapist is to alter the rigidity of the dialogue and to disconfirm the patient's distorted experience through attention to the process of sessions rather than the content of the interaction. The format is exclusively through time-limited group psychotherapy.

At first sight these three methods may sound distinctly different, ranging from individual therapy to a mix of individual and group therapy to solely group psychotherapy. Beyond that, there are some striking similarities. Both Kernberg and Linehan focus initial sessions on the establishment and negotiation of a treatment contract within the framework of their approach. A particular emphasis is placed on self-destructive behaviour, especially therapy-interfering behaviour, and appropriate limits are set and renewable contracts made. Both methods carefully define the responsibilities of the therapist on how self-destructive behaviour will be handled, regular appointments are arranged, and acceptance of difficulties of remaining in treatment is recognized and explicit statements made about the possibility of failure of treatment. Identity issues are central from a psychoanalytic viewpoint, and therapists are constantly on the alert for split-off aspects of patients and how these are played out in the patient–therapist relationship. In DBT there is less emphasis on identity issues, but nevertheless a "black-and-white" cognitive style is targeted through dialectical techniques to help the patient to overcome the all-or-none thinking and polarized approach to life. Both treatments prescribe the level of contact permissible between patient and therapist. In DBT, emergency sessions are allowed to enable the therapist and patient to develop alternative ways of crisis resolution, other than hospital admission or self-destructive behaviour. In psychoanalytic therapy contact between sessions is not permitted, although discussion of alternative routes to support between sessions may be a focus of a consultation. Implementation of the two treatments is consistent with theoretical views. Linehan provides information about cognitive–behavioural conceptualization of self-destructive behaviour, while Kernberg uses exploratory interpretations using ideographic hypotheses relating self-destructive behaviours to feelings about treatment. Both discuss alternative pathways to the resolution of conflict and distress.

In contrast to these overlaps, RMP takes a more neutral stance. No formal contract is made, no attempt is made to interpret or to explain the patient's anger or self-destructive behaviour, and no emphasis is given to education or understanding actions or threats that may disrupt therapy. Instead, the primary therapeutic task is to identify "core messages" that reflect the polarities of conflict about which the patient is struggling. Therapists generate hypotheses about these as they are played out in the group setting while avoiding enacting any of the externalized, polarized selves. On theoretical grounds, it may be supposed that this is the least supportive therapy for borderline patients and likely to lead to early drop-out or failure to take up offer of treatment, while DBT is the most supportive, given its methods and the availability of the therapist. While there are no data on the drop-out rate for RMP, Linehan has shown that the drop-out rate is low (16%) in DBT. While the drop-out rate for psychoanalytic therapy is reportedly higher, it may be altered. We (Bateman & Fonagy, 1999) had an attrition rate of only 12%.

The marked overlap between therapies for long-term treatment of personality disorder has significant implications for research, since randomized comparison of one intervention with another sits uppermost in a hierarchy of stringent tests for any treatment. Not only may this control for many processes independent of the treatment and common to all psychological treatments, but it may also include tests between specific competing mechanisms. But "horse-race" comparative studies in long-term treatment are unlikely to be helpful in identifying better methods of treatment, since there is so much variance within each treatment and overlap between them that differential treatment effects are likely to be masked. It is more important to isolate the effective aspects of different treatments (Waldinger & Gunderson, 1984). A decade on, it remains unclear what the effective components of DBT are. The original and unreplicated study was from a university department using highly trained and supervised therapists with enthusiasm and motivation implementing a new approach. Whether this can be generalized using less trained personnel working in community teams remains to be seen. Davidson and Tyrer (1996) remark that the translation of such a complex treatment into limited resource settings such as community mental health centres is questionable, given the many therapist hours and the requirement for expert supervision. Of course, this issue is not peculiar to DBT, and psychoanalytic treatments are probably poorly generalizable.

Conclusions from research

In the light of the considerable problems that still exist in conceptualizing and defining BPD, separating it from other mental disorders, and designing treatment trials of long-term therapy (which have adequate internal as well as external validity), it is perhaps not surprising that our knowledge concerning effective psychological treatments of BPD seems still to be somewhat rudimentary. Effective treatment protocols are relatively few in number and even where they exist remain largely untested. However, studies consistently demonstrate modest gains associated with relatively high doses of treatment. There is also encouraging evidence that these gains are cost effective (Gabbard, Lazar, Hornberger, & Spiegel, 1997; Stevenson, 1999), particularly in terms of savings in health care costs.

Halliwick Psychotherapy Unit: research and its implications

Our research demonstrates many of the problems that are outlined above. Both its strengths and weaknesses arise from the fact that it is clinical service research resulting in a trade-off between internal and external validity. On the positive side, firstly the programme was developed and implemented by a team of generically trained mental health professionals with an interest in psychoanalytically orientated psychiatry rather than by highly trained personnel within a university research department. Secondly, the research took place within a normal clinical setting and in a locality and healthcare system in which patients were unlikely to be able to obtain treatment elsewhere. The latter allowed effective tracing of patients within the service and accurate collection of data about psychiatric hospital admission. Thirdly patients were treated at only two local hospitals for medical emergencies such as self-harm, enabling us to obtain highly accurate data of episodes of self-harm requiring medical intervention. On the negative side, the programme was complex, leading to difficulty in being able to identify the effective ingredients should this be the result. It was also unfunded. However, the programme was designed so that it could be dismantled at a later date to determine the potent ingredients. At present a randomized controlled trial is underway of an outpatient treatment package made up of three of the ingredients that we consider to be the effective components of the programme.

In developing the research programme, we were joined by Peter Fonagy whose theoretical ideas and knowledge of research were pivotal in identifying a coherent treatment programme (Fonagy et al., 1992). Our initial tasks were to review the literature, to consider the evidence for effective interventions, and to match those to the skills within the team. We concluded that treatments shown to be effective with BPD had certain common features. They tended to

1. be well-structured;
2. devote considerable effort to the enhancing of compliance;
3. be clearly focused, whether that focus was a problem behaviour such as self-harm or an aspect of interpersonal relationship patterns;
4. be theoretically highly coherent to both therapist and patient, sometimes deliberately omitting information incompatible with the theory;
5. be relatively long-term;
6. encourage a powerful attachment relationship between therapist and patient, enabling the therapist to adopt a relatively active rather than a passive stance;
7. be well integrated with other services available to the patient.

While some of these features may be those of a successful research study rather than those of a successful therapy, we concluded that the manner in which treatment protocols were constructed and delivered was probably as important in the success of treatment as the theoretically driven interventions.

With these general features in mind, we set about developing a programme of treatment and organizing a research programme to test the effectiveness of the intervention. From the outset it was clear that this was to be "effectiveness research" rather than "efficacy" research—we would investigate the outcome of BPD treated by generically trained but non-specialist practitioners within a normal clinical setting. In this way, the treatment was more likely to be translatable to other NHS services without extensive and expensive additional training of personnel. But we had to first define a psychoanalytic view that was understandable to both staff and patients, then ensure that this enabled staff to think about any clinical situation that might arise, and, finally, define how to react in a consistent manner to common situations such as suicide threats and acts of self-harm.

Psychotherapy, BPD, attachment, and mentalizing

Psychotherapy, in all its incarnations, is about the rekindling of mentalization. Whether we look at Marsha Linehan's dialectic behaviour therapy protocol, John Clarkin's and Otto Kernberg's recommendations for psychoanalytic psychotherapy, or Anthony Ryle's cognitive analytic therapy, they all: (1) aim to establish an attachment relationship with the patient; (2) aim to use this to create an interpersonal context where understanding of mental states becomes a focus; (3) attempt—mostly implicitly—to recreate a situation where the self is recognized as intentional and real by the therapist and this recognition is clearly perceived by the patient.

The core of our treatment programme for BPD is to (1) help the patient understand and label emotional states with a view to strengthening the secondary representational system; (2) enhance reflective processes; (3) focus on brief, specific interpretation, initially avoiding a focus on aggression. Enhancement of reflective processes enables the development of stable internal representations and the formation of a coherent sense of self. Care about interpretation is important. For example, the inevitable destructiveness of these patients in relation to the therapeutic enterprise is rarely adequately dealt with by confrontation or interpretations of their aggressive intent. Such attacks are best regarded as self-protective.

Gaps in mentalization in BPD engender impulsivity, and during treatment the intensification of the therapeutic relationship highlights the patient's difficulties and further exposes the rift between internal and external reality. This stimulates enactments. Attempts to bridge this dissociated mode of a patient's functioning, where nothing feels real—certainly not words or ideas—to moments when words and ideas carry unbelievable potency and destructiveness can seem an awesome task. The therapist's concern is in some way analogous to that of the parents who create a frame for pretend play—except in this case it is thoughts and feelings that need to become accessible through the creation of a transitional area. The therapist must get used to working with precursors of mentalization. The task is the elaboration of teleological models into intentional ones (Dennett, 1987). Yet it is only by being able to become part of the patient's pretend world, trying to make it real while at the same time avoiding entanglement with the equation of thoughts and reality, that progress becomes conceivable. In our view, this process is best done within a transference–countertransference relationship, but by a team of professionals rather than by an individual working alone because of the severe difficulty in avoiding destructive entanglements.

Transference

Whatever the approach taken to the treatment of BPD, problems of transference and countertransference are inevitably present and need to be planned for. Even in DBT, supervision takes into account the feelings engendered in the therapist by that patient and how such feelings can distract the therapist from his task. But should the psychoanalytic therapist work in the transference with borderline patients?

The transference of early relationship patterns onto current relationships, while ever-present, is rarely helpful to highlight. Without mentalization, which acts as a buffer between internal and external reality, transference is not displacement but is experienced as real. If the therapist is experienced as an abuser, he *is* the abuser—no "as-if" about it. When such transference interpretations are made, the patient is often thrown into confusion, and to protect the therapy, has no choice but to enter a pretend mode in which their subjective experience has no relationship to what is perceived by the therapist as reality (Fonagy & Target, 1996). Gradually patient and therapist may elaborate a world that, however detailed and complex, has little experiential contact with anything that feels real. In our view transference interpretation has to be more circumspect and is best dismantled into small parts that build up over time in an incremental way. For example, a simple acknowledgement of affect in the here and now, while conveying in words, tone, and posture that the therapist is able to cope with the patient's emotional state, may be the most productive line initially. Generic transference interpretation should be used—if ever in its raw form—only late in treatment. Transference, using the term in its broadest sense, is helpful as a concrete demonstration of alternative perspectives. The contrast between the patient's perception of the therapist as she or he is imagined and as she or he actually is may help to place quotation marks around the transference experience.

Some programmes attempt to control enactments by making therapy contractually dependent. In our day-hospital and outpatient programme we do not make "therapy-dependent" contracts. To do so risks discharging the patient for the very problems for which they are being treated. Being modest in one's aims is the most helpful device. One should not hope that insight through interpretation of transference will prevent enactment; the aim is simply the gradual encouragement of mentalization. Consequently, the interpretation of enactments is rarely as helpful as trying to deal with their antecedents and consequences. We need to be equally permissive about our own tendency to enact in the countertransference. We have to accept that in order for the patient to stay in mental proximity, we have to become what they need us to be. Yet we know that if we become that person, we can be of no help to them. Our aim should be the achievement of a state of equipoise between the two—allowing oneself to do as required yet trying to retain in our mind as clear and as coherent an image of the state of the mind of the patient as we are able to achieve.

Split transference

One of the most complicated challenges arising from treating BPD relates to externalizations of unbearable self-states. Splitting the transference by creating alternative foci for the patient's feelings is important here. In our programme the transference is split in a number of ways. First, a package of group and individual therapy splits the transference and allows the patient to reflect on himself in the group during the individual session. Second, patients with BPD commonly have severe social problems or trouble with the law, and so an additional member of the team is appointed to help them deal with these practical realities while the individual therapist focuses on the relationship problems, unencumbered by practical issues.

So, what are the hallmarks of a successful therapy with an individual with severe borderline features?

No theory gets anywhere close to explaining the complex problems of this group of patients. However, having a theoretically coherent approach is vital. Such patients require that we are predictable, and our implicit working models of them can then begin to form the core of their self-representations. A stable, coherent image is impossible to maintain if the therapist swaps theoretical approaches at an alarming rate. Mentalization can only be acquired in the context of an attachment relationship. This means that the therapy must embody a secure base. Attachment is inseparable from a focus on the mental state of the other. There can be no bond without understanding, even if understanding is possible without a bond. Treatment always takes considerable time, and consistency over such prolonged periods is often difficult to maintain. The patient is terrified of and actively fights mental closeness, even when physical proximity appears to be his overarching goal. Retaining such proximity while under persistent attack is neither comfortable nor likely to be achieved unless one leaves one's personal sensitivity at the door. Finally, one should be careful not to under-estimate the extent of the patient's incapacity. It is easy and relatively comforting to engage with the representational world of these patients at a level of complexity that they, in reality, have little appreciation of. They are readily seduced into such relationships and accept these complexities within a pretend mode, dramatically removed from anything that feels real to them. Such therapies tend to be durable, but they are sadly unhelpful in the long run.

In order to establish consistency within a secure base and to minimize entanglement within transference and countertransference enactments, we take a team approach. The team's mentalistic, elaborative stance ultimately enables the patient to find himself in the team's mind as a thinking, feeling being. This allows him to integrate this image as part of his sense of himself. There is a gradual transformation of a non-reflective mode of experiencing the internal world that forces the equation of the internal and external into one in which the internal world is treated with more circumspection and respect and as separate and qualitatively different from physical reality. Even if work were to stop here, much would have been achieved in terms of making behaviour understandable, meaningful, and predictable. The internalization of the team's concern with mental states enhances the patient's capacity for similar concern towards his own experience. Respect for minds generates respect for self, respect for other, and, ultimately, respect for the human community. It is this respect that drives and organizes the therapeutic endeavour within our programme, and it is the operationalization of these ideas that we put to the test.

Research and results

In the present study, we carried out a randomization of patients either to treatment in the day-hospital programme or to continuing treatment within the general psychiatric service (control group). All patients were assessed using standardized criteria for BPD, namely the Structured Clinical Interview for the DSM–III–R

(SCID–II) (Spitzer et al., 1990) and the Diagnostic Interview for Borderlines (DIB) (Gunderson, Kolb, & Austin, 1981). A cut-off score of 7 or more was used for a formal diagnosis of BPD. If patients met both criteria for BPD, they were selected for randomization either to treatment in the day-hospital programme or to continuing psychiatric treatment. Patients were excluded from the study if they also met DSM–III–R, based on SCID–I, criteria for schizophrenia, bipolar disorder, substance misuse, or mental impairment, or had evidence of organic brain disorder based on SCID–I (Spitzer et al., 1990). The criteria for inclusion in the study were met by 60 referrals; 10 refused to participate in the randomization; 6 of these were admitted to the day-hospital programme and excluded from the present study; 4 declined further treatment of any type; and 6 further patients did not wish to participate in regular self-assessment and so were also not included. This process of randomization sounds easy, but in fact borderline patients change their minds about research on a regular basis, and it becomes increasingly difficult to ensure that patients are clear about their decisions. However, when everything was sorted out, there were no significant differences on any of the baseline measures for patients who did not participate in the study compared with the 44 patients who did enter the study, who were randomly assigned to the two groups. Within the first month of entering the study, three control patients crossed over into the day-hospital programme following serious suicide attempts leading to inpatient medical and psychiatric treatment. Three patients (12%) in the day-hospital group dropped out of treatment within six months. All were available for follow-up. No subjects dropped out of the control group. Demographic and clinical characteristics of the total cohort of patients are described in the original paper. Following randomization, there were no significant differences on any variable between the two groups, including frequencies or average number of Axis I and Axis II disorders. Particularly notable was the association of mood and anxiety disorders with BPD.

Treatment in the day-hospital condition consisted of:

1. once-weekly individual psychoanalytic psychotherapy;
2. three times per week group analytic psychotherapy lasting an hour each;

3. once-a-week expressive therapy informed by psychodrama techniques (one hour);

4. weekly community meeting (one hour)

all spread over five days. In addition, on a once-per-month basis, subjects had

5. a meeting with the case-administrator (one hour);

6. medication review by the resident psychiatrist.

Therapies and informal patient–staff contact were organized in accordance with a psychoanalytic model of BPD, as described above. Medication consisted of antidepressant and anti-psychotic drugs prescribed as appropriate; polypharmacy was discouraged. The maximum length of treatment was set at eighteen months.

All therapy was given by psychiatrically trained nurse members of the day-hospital team with no formal psychotherapy qualifications. Adherence to therapy was monitored through supervision (twice a week with the whole team) using verbatim session reports and by completion of a monitoring form collecting information about activities and interventions of therapists. Aspects of the day-hospital programme have been described elsewhere (Bateman, 1995, 1997).

We chose "treatment as usual" in the general psychiatric service as control treatment. This consisted of

1. regular psychiatric review with the senior psychiatrist when necessary (twice per month on average);

2. inpatient admission as appropriate (admission rate 90%, average duration 11.6 days) with discharge to non-psychoanalytic psychiatric day-hospital treatment focusing on problem solving (72% attended day hospital, with average length of stay of six months); followed by

3. outpatient and community follow-up (100%, fortnightly by CPN visits) as standard aftercare.

None of the control group received any formal psychotherapy. The initial types and doses of medication were the same for both groups. While this group cannot be considered to have received the amount of professional attention comparable to that given to the day-hospital group, the approach controls for spontaneous remission.

Measures of outcome

We used a series of self-report measures, but only the effectiveness of the programme in reducing suicide attempts and other acts of self-harm, decreasing hospital admissions, and ameliorating depression are considered here.

Acts of self-harm and clinical measures

The criteria for suicidal acts were: (1) deliberate; (2) life-threatening; (3) had resulted in medical intervention; (4) medical assessment was consistent with a suicide attempt. Criteria for acts of self-mutilation were: (1) deliberate; (2) resulting in visible tissue damage; (3) nursing or medical intervention required.

A semi-structured interview (Suicide and Self-Harm Inventory) was used to obtain details of both suicidal and self-damaging acts for the six-month period before patients entered the study. This interview asks specific questions not only about numbers of acts but also about dangerousness of acts—that is, presence or absence of another person, likelihood of being found, preparation, and lethality. Multiple acts over a short period of time—for example, a frenzied self-cutting—were counted as a single act. Day-hospital patients were monitored carefully with regard to self-destructive acts, and control patients were interviewed every six months. Self-reports of suicidal and self-mutilatory acts were cross-checked with medical and psychiatric notes.

For all patients, a search of the hospital inpatient database was made to obtain the number of hospital admissions and the length of stay during a period of six months before entry into the study. This was cross-checked with the medical notes. All patients were admitted to the local unit because of the contracted nature of the service. Hospital admission and length of stay as well as psychiatric day-hospital programme attendance were monitored throughout the study for all patients.

Follow-up

An attempt was made eighteen months following admission to follow all 44 patients for an additional eighteen months. No patient in the partial hospitalization programme was lost to follow-up, but some refused to complete all assessments at all time-points. Three patients in the control group refused continued participation. Complete medical records were, however, available for these patients. While assessments were not blind, all the outcome variables were based on objective clinical records confirmed by independent evaluation or were self-report measures.

Details were collected of both suicidal and self-damaging acts at the 24-, 30-, and 36-month evaluations. For all patients, searches of the hospital inpatient database were made at the 24-, 30-, and 36-month evaluations to obtain the number of hospital admissions and the lengths of stay over the preceding six months.

It was not possible to prevent patients having further treatment. Participation in other treatment programmes was monitored throughout the study for all patients, including medication data ascertained from prescription charts and dispensing records. A follow-up programme was offered to the patients assigned to the partial hospitalization programme, which was attended by all except the three who prematurely terminated treatment. The programme consisted of group analytic therapy twice a week (180 hours over eighteen months) and review in a psychiatric outpatient clinic, if requested, every three months. Group attendance was 75% during the follow-up period, which indicates the stability of this cohort of treated patients. Community centre attendance and general psychiatric partial hospitalization programmes were available through self-referral. The control group continued their general psychiatric treatment, which could involve inpatient admission when required, a general psychiatric partial hospitalization programme, outpatient consultation, community centre attendance, or medication. None received any formal psychotherapy, although this was not precluded during the follow-up period.

Results

Detailed results can be found in our two published papers (Bateman & Fonagy, 1999, 2001), and only some points of particular interest are discussed here.

Depression

Our treatment programme made little difference to self-reported symptoms of depression as measured by the Beck Depression Inventory (Beck et al., 1961) for six months, but following that period a continual decline in depressive symptoms was noted. At discharge only three treated subjects and no controls were below the clinical cut-off point on the BDI. The proportion scoring below 14 increased over the follow-up period to 59% by eighteen months in the treated group, but only to 12.5% in the controls (Figure 6.1).

This is in contrast to the RCT of dialectical behaviour therapy, in which there were no changes in levels of depression either at the end of treatment or during follow-up. It seems that the psychoanalytically oriented programme stimulates rehabilitative effects, but a

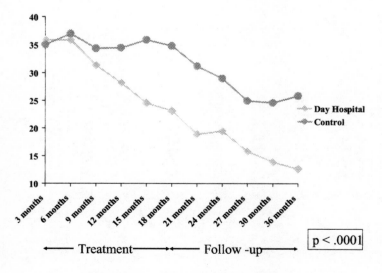

Figure 6.1 Self-rated depression (Beck).

cognitive behavioural programme focusing on symptoms and skills does not. This argument is further supported by the results of suicide and self-harm during follow-up.

Suicide and self-harm

The continual decline throughout follow-up in suicide attempts and acts of self-harm in the treated group compared with the control group is testament to the rehabilitative effects of the programme (Figures 6.2 and 6.3). Throughout the study and follow-up period there were no successful suicides in either group, and the rapid decrease in suicide attempts during the first six months of treatment suggests that simply offering patients a structured, coherent programme of treatment may suffice to reduce their dangerous behaviour. The slower effect on self-harm, with a significant change occurring after one year, suggests either that our programme did not focus adequately on such acts (it does not specifically target self-harm alone) or that understanding the meaning of self-laceration in terms of interpersonal and affective contexts takes time to have an effect on such symptoms as a way of dealing with anxiety.

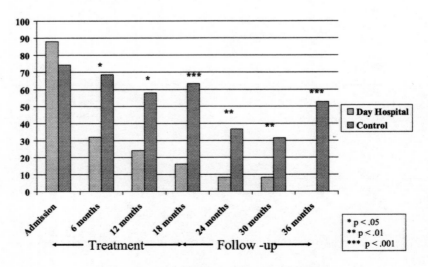

Figure 6.2. Percentage of attempted suicides.

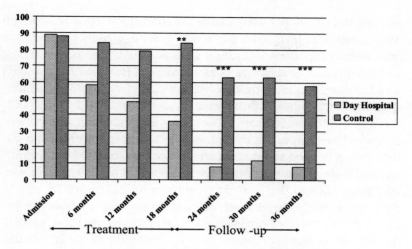

Figure 6.3. Percentage of self-mutilating behaviour.

Psychiatric admissions

The average length of hospitalization throughout treatment and follow-up, adjusted for pre-admission values, is displayed in Figure 6.4 This confirms that average length of hospitalization in the control group in the last six months of the study increased dramatically, whereas in the PH group it remained relatively stable at

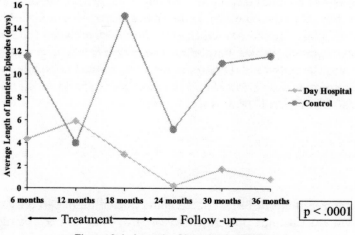

Figure 6.4. Length of inpatient episodes.

around four days per six months. The Group × Time interaction was significant [$F(1, 35) = 7.7$, $p < .01$], with a highly significant quadratic component [$F(1, 35) = 13.3$, $p < .001$]. The post-hoc test yielded significant differences at six months [$t(36) = 7.66$, $p < .001$] and at eighteen months [$t(36) = 13.23$, $p < .001$]. An identical pattern emerged for number of inpatient episodes [$F(1, 35) = 14.1$, $p < .001$; $F(1, 35) = 19.9$, $p < .001$ for the two-way and quadratic component of the interaction, respectively]. In the day-hospital group no patient was admitted six months after discharge, but one was admitted for 20 days one year after discharge and a further patient was admitted twice in the final six months of follow-up for 25 and 12 days, respectively. In contrast, in the control group, 7 patients were admitted at least once during the first six months after discharge, 7 during the second six months, and 14 during the final six months. These differences were all significant on Fisher's Exact Test ($p < .002$, $p < .02$, $p < .001$ for six, twelve, and eighteen-month time-points of follow-up, respectively). The average number of days in hospital increased from 6 ($SD = 10.8$, range 0 to 28) in the first six months of the follow-up period, to 12.7 ($SD = 19.4$, range 0 to 65) in the second, and 15.8 ($SD = 12.9$, range 0 to 40) in the final six months of the follow-up. The differences were significant at all time points on the Mann-Whitney test ($U = 143$, $n = 41$, $p < .005$; $U = 138$, $n = 41$, $p < .007$; $U = 72$, $n = 41$, $p < .001$ for six, twelve, and eighteen months, respectively). As there was little variation in the number of hospital days in the day-hospital group, we only examined trends in the control group. The repeated-measures ANOVA on this group indicated significant differences between time points of assessment [Wilk's Lambda = .644, $F(2, 16) = 4.18$, $p < .03$]. Exploring the polynomial components of this effect confirmed a significant quadratic effect [$F(1, 17) = 5.60$, $p < .03$] and no significant linear effect [$F(1, 17) < 1$, n.s.].

Conclusions

In the treatment of BPD, effectiveness of treatment can only really be shown through prolonged follow-up. BPD is a relapsing and remitting problem, with individuals showing periods of reasonable function followed by episodes of chaos and disorder. Only prolonged follow-up can determine whether greater stability has been achieved. Our study has one of the longest follow-up periods of a randomized controlled trial of treatment. An uncontrolled study of psychoanalytically orientated treatment by Stevenson and Meares (1992, 1995) has data from a five-year follow-up. Both follow-up studies show that the initial gains found at the end of treatment are maintained during follow-up. Howard's interesting conceptualization of psychotherapy into three phases is helpful in understanding this. He suggested that psychotherapy process could be understood as first showing a period of remoralization, then remediation, and, finally, rehabilitation. Remoralization or a reduction in distress tends to occur quickly, and some of the early changes in our patients, such as the decrease in general symptom distress, were possibly a result of remoralization. Remediation involves refocusing the patients' coping skills and helping them to see their problems from a different perspective. This is, of course, a major aspect of our programme as we attempt to increase mentalization and identification and self-control of affect. It is during this time that patients realize that their problems result from longstanding patterns that are maladaptive and unconsciously determined, and that there are no quick fixes. But the real test of treatment is whether or not there are any rehabilitative effects of the programme, and this is only determined by follow-up. Do patients who have made gains at the end of treatment maintain those gains? Can they cope with the everyday stresses and strains of life without engaging in their previous strategies of self-harm, and so on? Our results suggest that this is the case. Not only are the gains made at the end of treatment maintained, but there are also further improvements. This is particularly clear in the results of depression, suicide attempts, and self-harm, and in psychiatric admissions.

While the results of our study are encouraging, we know neither why patients improve, nor which patients are likely to benefit most from a psychoanalytically orientated treatment. Further development of psychoanalytic approaches to the treatment of BPD will only come about if we identify the mechanisms of therapeutic change more precisely and decide on the sequencing of interventions and on whom the interventions are to be carried out. If psychoanalysis is to remain a vibrant and living discipline, further research is urgently needed. Only if this takes place will a psychoanalytically based treatment of BPD have a central place in the twenty-first century.

CHAPTER SEVEN

Henderson Hospital democratic therapeutic community: outcome studies and methodological issues

Fiona Warren & Kingsley Norton

History of Henderson Hospital

Henderson Hospital is a democratic therapeutic community based in South London. It was set up in 1947 by Dr Maxwell Jones, one of the pioneers of therapeutic community developments within the United Kingdom. The aptly named "Industrial Neurosis Unit" was started on an experimental basis, with the implicit assumption that its utility required evaluation. In establishing the unit, the then Ministry of Labour's aim was to help to resettle "the industrial misfit" following the Second World War (Whiteley, 1980). The idea behind the experiment was simple: if during the war a useful place had been found for society's social and psychological casualties, it should also be possible in peacetime for them to be helped to find resources within themselves to lead more useful and fulfilling lives.

Over time, the patient group, treatment methods, and aims and objectives of the Unit changed, as did its name. It became the Social Rehabilitation Unit in 1954, in acknowledgement that the inability of many to settle in a job was due more to their lack of social skills than to industrial or educational expertise. Patients were increasingly referred via the courts, rehabilitation offices, or social work agencies to which they had drifted and where they had become labelled as social inadequates. By the mid-1950s the Unit was recognized as a centre specializing in therapeutic community ideology and the treatment of "psychopaths" (Whiteley, 1980). In 1959, the Unit was again renamed—Henderson Hospital—when it became independent of its large parent hospital—Belmont Hospital. Its naming honoured Professor D. K. Henderson, author of *Psychopathic States* (Henderson, 1939).

Over the ensuing four decades, the Henderson Hospital approach has stabilized, maintaining an equilibrium that continues to address the therapeutic needs of its severely personality-disordered clientele, despite periodic threats to its survival resulting from its highly specialist (and unusual) status. The treatment has been described in increasingly greater detail, enhancing the chances that the treatment approach could be replicated and the generalizability of its outcome findings evaluated (Norton, 1992a, 1992b, 1995, 1996; Whiteley, 1986), and, more recently, the hospital has collaborated with two other UK Mental Health NHS trusts (South Birmingham and Mental Health Services of Salford) in an attempt to replicate the model.

Henderson Hospital today

The aim of much of the integrated socio- and psychotherapy programme can be summarized as converting people who "act", rather than thinking or feeling, into individuals who are able to sustain and recognize their feelings and begin to articulate their psychological needs (Norton & Dolan, 1995a). Maintaining this approach throughout 24 hours per day is problematic, entailing, as it does, staff working in close collaboration with the patients themselves (Norton & Hinshelwood, 1996). Achieving this overall aim necessarily involves staff in an ongoing set of transference–countertransference relationships with patients, which spans (potentially) 24 hours of the day (Whiteley, 1986). This psychodynamic situation requires an elaborate set of supportive and supervisory structures for staff in order for them to sustain, reflect on, and process their countertransference reactions (Rosenbluth, 1991). With this kind of client group, such activity is extremely important in minimizing the destructive effects of any inter-staff splitting and promoting a therapeutic culture (Main, 1957; Norton & Hinshelwood, 1996).

Early literature on the TC suggested various definitions that may still be seen to underlie the approach today. Hence, for Main it was the idea of the full participation of all its members in its daily life that characterized the TC (Main, 1946). For Maxwell Jones, the TC implied that the responsibility for the treatment was not confined to trained staff but also to other community members, including the patients (Jones, 1952). Perhaps Main captured the democratic TC's essence in referring to it as a "culture of enquiry" (Main, 1983). This idea has been developed further (Norton, 1992a).

The past: retrospective outcome studies

Social criteria of successful treatment include clinical improvement, employment, reconviction, and readmission to psychiatric facilities.

Clinical improvement

The Rapoport team, brought together to study the Belmont Social Rehabilitation Unit, intended to evaluate the treatment programme—an evaluation that critics of Maxwell Jones and his method were calling for (Rapoport, 1960). However, there was controversy over the diagnostic use of the term "psychopath", and, partly because of this, the study changed direction, becoming more an in-depth exploration of the workings of the community than an outcome study (Whiteley, 1980). The overall study period spanned four years (1953 to 1957) (Manning & Rapoport, 1976; Rapoport, 1960).

A small-scale outcome study was incorporated, however, and the findings suggested that the democratic therapeutic community method was not universally applicable, that some selection process for patients was necessary, and that the intensive social and interpersonal pressures could damage those with weak ego structures. Rapoport had also pointed out a conflict of aims between those of the therapeutic staff and those of the workshop instructors who were aiming for "rehabilitation". The findings were largely viewed negatively by the Unit's staff, and Maxwell Jones himself left the Unit in 1959 (Whiteley, 1980).

For the outcome study, one year after discharge Rapoport's team personally interviewed and classified 64 patients according to whether they were "improved", "same", or "worse" compared to when they had entered the Unit. On the stated criteria, 41% were considered improved, 18% unchanged, and 31% worse. Improvement was associated with longer duration in treatment: 52% for those staying more than 200 days were judged improved. No objective measures were used, nor were any comparison samples studied.

Reoffending, employment, and responsibility

In a later outcome study—a postal survey of the probation officers of 86 consecutive male discharges, on probation or borstal licences—62% of those traced were free of further convictions, up to twenty-two months post-discharge (Tuxford, 1961). The response rate of the study was 84%. Assessment was made using a 4-point scale completed by the probation officer, ranging from 1 (increased sense of responsibility, employment and no further offending) to 4 (further offending, unemployment and lack of responsibility): 24% fell into the first category, 31% into the second, 28% were in the "poor outcome" category, and 17% were considered as complete treatment failures (Dolan & Coid, 1993). Overall, this represented a 55% success rate, on the assessment criteria.

A similar rate of success was found in a follow-up study of discharged men (number unknown) who were assessed nine months post-discharge (Taylor, 1963): 22% had found their own employment, and a further 47% had been placed in employment with professional support. The latter group was followed up for a further nine months, and 60% of these were still in work with a satisfactory report from their employers.

Of 122 discharged men, 40% had no further psychiatric admission or conviction at two-year follow-up (Whiteley, 1970). Of men with previous convictions, over 40% remained free of convictions. Of those with previous admissions to a psychiatric hospital, almost 60% remained out of hospital over the two-year period. Good prognostic factors were: some level of school achievement; ever sustaining employment for more than two years; higher social-class occupation; ever having been married; and a history of affective disorder. A negative outcome was associated with: having previous convictions; prior prison sentence(s); a probation order at referral or admission; current court proceedings; and institutionalization before the age of 15.

A further outcome study was undertaken to develop a prediction equation for successful outcome (Copas & Whiteley, 1976). Two cohorts of male patients were studied. One cohort of 104, at two years, showed 42% as having no further convictions or readmissions, while the cohort of 87 revealed a slightly higher figure of 47% successful outcome on these criteria. At five years follow-up of the 104, one third had no reconviction or readmission, and a further 11% had only minor relapses in the first year of follow-up, remaining free of conviction or relapse in the succeeding four years. It could be considered, therefore, that 45% of the total had a good outcome.

None of these early outcome studies utilized any comparison groups, making it impossible to conclude that improvements were attributable to Henderson Hospital's democratic therapeutic community. However, a five-year follow-up study of 194 (male and female) patients was carried out, which also reported on 51 patients referred to Henderson but not admitted (Copas, O'Brien, Roberts, & Whiteley, 1984). Similar criteria of success were utilized. At three years, 41% of the treated sample was improved compared to 23% of the non-admitted. At five years, the relative proportions were 36% and 19%. There was no significant gender difference. Further analysis of these findings showed a positive association between success rate and length of stay in treatment. At three years' follow-up, 62% of those who had stayed for six months and

71% of those staying for nine months were improved. At five years, the relevant proportions were 57% and 65% for six- and nine-months' stays, compared with 19% of those not admitted (i.e. having treatment as usual elsewhere).

Psychological criteria: neurotic symptomatology

Reconviction and readmission to psychiatric facilities are often used as outcomes but are only indirect measures of psychological health. These earlier studies of outcome (measured mainly in terms of further conviction or psychiatric hospitalization) were later complemented by the undertaking of a study of psychological morbidity (Dolan, Evans, & Wilson, 1992) as measured by the SCL–90–R (Derogatis, Rickels, & Rock, 1976). A total of 62 subjects were followed up at an average of eight months post-discharge, and findings revealed a highly significant improvement post-discharge on the Global Symptom Index (i.e. total score on SCL–90–R). Again, this was not a controlled study, and the numbers were relatively small, although representing a typical figure for the number of patients treated in a given year.

The SCL–90–R is a self-rated instrument. However, data were subjected to a rigorous statistical analysis, addressing both the issue of reliability and also the importance of the observed clinical change (Jacobson & Truax, 1991). With this method, 55% of the group had improved reliably (i.e. had moved two standard deviations in relation to their baseline score). In 32%, the change was clinically significant (i.e. subjects no longer scored in the pathological range but had scores within the normal range for the measure, defined by reference to normative data published on the instrument). Only 6.5% had deteriorated reliably.

In this sample, length of stay was not significantly related to outcome, although those who had stayed for longer than nine months did show greater or more beneficial change than those who had stayed less (mean improvement = .73, $SD = 0.84$, for the longer-stay vs. mean improvement = .58, $SD = .86$, for the medium-stay, and mean improvement = .61, $SD = 1.1$, for the short-stay groups). However, gender was significantly related to length of stay, with more women staying longer than nine months (23/44, 52%, vs. 12/51, 29%, chi-squared 4.24, $p = .04$).

The present: prospective outcome study

In 1990, a large prospective outcome study was launched by the then single-handed researcher, Dr Bridget Dolan, who was at the time based solely at the hospital, with no other formal academic links. Given the slender resources, this was an ambitious project. The study attempted to produce a psychological profile of all referrals during the study period. In addition, it aimed to rate all patients admitted at three-monthly intervals and at one and three years post-discharge, and those not admitted at one and three years post-referral. At this time there was no published large-scale prospective study in the field of personality disorder, and the proposed study was breaking new ground in terms of improved research methodology.

Shortly after the study began, in 1991, major changes to the United Kingdom's National Health Service took place. In effect, service provision of the NHS was separated organizationally from its purchasing. As a consequence of the changes, local districts became more responsible for identifying the health needs of "their" catchment-area populations and using their funding allocation from central government to purchase these. Henderson's national catchment area meant that its funding depended on referrals other than from its local catchment area (extra-contractual referrals—ECR). Henderson's client group did not compete well with other extra-contractual referrals in the new "market-place" (Dolan & Coid, 1994).

The numbers of applications for admission that attracted funding decreased, and the financial viability of the hospital was threatened as, in the minds of purchasers, the treatment was not considered of proven worth but an expensive luxury that the NHS could no longer afford. Paradoxically, two research benefits emerged from this otherwise negative scenario: (1) A study of cost-offset was evoked in order to challenge the "expensive" price tag

(Dolan, Warren, Menzies, & Norton, 1996; Menzies, Dolan, & Norton, 1993); (2) a group of referrals emerged who did not get admitted for treatment solely because the health authority refused to fund their extra-contractual referrals (ECR). This, it could be argued, provided a comparison group closer to a randomly allocated control than the whole group of non-admitted referrals, for whom non-admission may have resulted from characteristics also relevant to treatment outcome (Dolan, Warren, & Norton, 1997).

Cost as a measure of outcome

Two papers report the cost-offset of Henderson treatment. In the first study, service usage data were collected retrospectively from May 1992 on 29 consecutive admissions, and success rates of previously published outcome studies were used to calculate cost-offset. In the second study, actual service usage in the one-year post-treatment was used to calculate the actual cost-offset for these admissions.

Data on mental health and forensic service usage in the one year prior to admission to Henderson derived from three sources: (1) case notes, including information provided by the referrer; (2) the "Social History Form", a questionnaire completed by all admissions, concerning family, personal, and clinical history; (3) subjects who were resident during the study period completed an additional form about the previous year's usage of services. Costs were calculated by obtaining figures of ECR tariffs for 1992/93 from the then four Thames Regional Health Authorities (RHA).

The daily tariff for Henderson Hospital was £111, compared with £153.20 for a general acute psychiatric bed and £173 for Close Supervision Units. The 29 Henderson admissions had used a considerable amount of health and prison services during the previous year: the average estimated costs had been £423,115 per year (mean cost per patient = £14,590). In this first study, the cost of treatment at Henderson was offset by extrapolating from the 41% success rate in the studies reviewed above. This suggested that the treatment would pay for itself in four years (Menzies, Dolan, & Norton, 1993).

Subsequently, in the second study, follow-up information had been obtained in the course of the prospective outcome study on actual service usage for 24 (83%) of the 29 residents in the original sample (Menzies, Dolan, & Norton, 1993). The average cost of services used by these 24 residents in the one year prior to admission had been £13,966.

Information on service usage in the one year subsequent to discharge from Henderson was obtained from their referrer (in 17 cases) and/or their general practitioner (GP) (in 14 cases) and from the client themselves (in 7 cases). Of the patients, 4 had further inpatient admissions, 1 of whom was re-admitted to the Henderson; 2 had outpatient assessments, 12 had outpatient treatment, and 1 attended a day hospital. None of the residents spent time in prison or a secure psychiatric unit during the year. The average cost of services used was £1,308. This represents an annual saving post-discharge of £12,658.

These 24 residents were in treatment at Henderson Hospital for an average of 231 days (range 1–365 days); thus the actual cost of their treatment at Henderson was £25,641. Should the cost-offset continue at a similar rate for subsequent years, then the cost of admission to Henderson would be recouped in less than two years and represent savings thereafter.

Borderline symptoms as a measure of outcome

Reviewing outcome studies in the field of personality disorder (Norton & Dolan, 1995b), many studies fail to assess the impact of treatment on aspects intrinsic to the personality disorder pathology itself, separately from those that are only associated or indirect phenomena. Indeed, there is a range of features associated with personality disorder, changes in which are erroneously equated with change in the personality disorder itself, such as reduction in Axis I diagnosis symptomatology, or behavioural features such as criminal activity, self-mutilation, or suicidality. This prospective study aimed to assess changes in core personality disorder features. Comparison was made between those admitted and those not admitted for treatment. Consecutive referrals were mailed a self-report questionnaire pack on referral, including the Personality Disorder Questionnaire (PDQ-R) (Hyler, Reider, & Spitzer, 1987), the Borderline Syndrome Index (BSI) (Conte, Plutchik,

Karasu, & Vaccaro, 1980), the Irritability, Depression and Anxiety Scale (IDA) (Snaith, Constantopoulos, Jardine, & McGuffin, 1978), and the Rosenberg Self-Esteem Scale (RSE) (Rosenberg, 1965). A second follow-up assessment pack was sent one year after referral (for the not admitted) or discharge (for the admitted group). Up to three repeated mailings were used to maximize response rate.

The results of this study showed a significantly greater reduction in BSI scores in the treated than in the non-admitted group (Dolan, Warren, & Norton, 1997). Changes in BSI scores were significantly positively correlated with length of treatment in the admitted group. Again, assessment of the reliability and clinical significance (Jacobson & Truax, 1991) of changes in individual subjects was conducted in this study. These showed that the magnitude of this change was reliable and clinically significant in 42.9% of the admitted sample, compared with only 17.9% of the non-admitted sample (18.2% of the unfunded group).

Mood as a measure of outcome: work in progress

Given the positive effects shown on borderline symptomatology, the outcome in terms of mood was also of interest in the prospective outcome study. Depression, anxiety, and inwardly and outwardly directed irritability were assessed using the IDA (Snaith et al., 1978) on the same cohort of patients. This instrument was chosen because it covers relevant symptoms theoretically related to personality disorder—anxiety and depression—and, in addition, assesses the socially relevant tendencies to hurt the self or others. The 18-item scale is scored from 0 to 4; the depression and anxiety subscales are scored between 0 and 15, and the irritability scales are scored between 0 and 12.

Participants

Response rates

The study sample is derived from the sample on which borderline symptoms were reported by Dolan, Warren, and Norton

(1997). However, the study period was extended; therefore the sample and response rates are summarized here. Consecutive referrals to the service between September 1990 and December 1994 were approached to participate in the study. There were 585 eligible referrals in the study period, of whom 384 (66%) completed a baseline assessment; 12 (3%) of these were excluded from follow-up because they were re-referred for treatment in the period between initial and follow-up assessment. Of the remaining 372 eligible participants, 135 (36%), responded at follow-up assessment; of these, 75 (56%) were admitted and 60 (44%) were not admitted.

Demographic characteristics

The mean age of the sample was 28 (range = 17 to 49, SD = 6.8), with just under one half female. Almost all the sample was white, single, and unemployed. A large proportion had been previously convicted and had histories of drug and alcohol abuse. High rates of previous suicide attempts, self-mutilation, and overdosing were also reported by the referrers.

Personality disorder

This sample is a severely personality-disordered group of people (Dolan, Evans, & Norton, 1995). The mean number of personality disorders for which each individual met criteria was seven, and 95% of the sample met criteria for more than one personality disorder. Two cases did not score above threshold for any personality disorder, and one case had missing data. The mean PDQ–R total score was 58 (see Table 7.1). Of these participants, 84% met criteria for BPD.

Table 7.2 shows the prevalence of personality disorder diagnoses. Following borderline, the most common diagnoses are paranoid, schizotypal, and avoidant. The two research categories (self-defeating and sadistic) are the least prevalent. The most prevalent diagnoses were spread across the putative clusters into which personality disorder diagnoses are grouped in DSM–III–R and DSM–IV. Each cluster contained at least one score for over 80%

Table 7.1. Personality disorder symptoms: breadth and number of diagnoses

	Participants	%	Mean	Range	SD
Total	n = 134				
PDQ-R total score			57.49	17–86	13.00
Number of diagnoses[a]			6.80	0–12	2.94
More than one diagnosis	n = 127	94.8			

[a] The research categories are included, so this is the number of diagnoses out of a possible 13.

of the group. Over 70% of the participants met criteria for personality disorders in all three clusters. There was a slightly higher proportion of schizoid personality disorder in the admitted than in the non-admitted group.

Table 7.2. Personality disorder sub-category diagnoses

Sub-category diagnoses	Percentage admitted (n = 74)	Percentage not admitted (n = 60)
Paranoid	77	65
Schizoid	55	33*
Schizotypal	74	62
Antisocial	58	67
Borderline	82	85
Histrionic	55	67
Narcissistic	39	40
Avoidant	69	62
Obsessive	47	38
Dependent	62	52
Passive-aggressive	47	33
Self-defeating	14	22
Sadistic	22	27

* significant at $p < .05$

Representativeness

Given the naturalistic nature of this study and the attrition of participants over time, tests were conducted to establish the representativeness of the sample. Group differences at baseline suggested that outcome analyses should take sex and the presence of schizoid personality disorder into consideration.

Length of stay

The average length of stay of the admitted participants in this comparison was 201 days (6.7 months). The minimum length of stay was two days and the maximum 396.

Outcomes

The results of repeated-measures ANOVA are summarized in Table 7.3. The table shows the baseline and follow-up mean score for each group and the interaction effect. The BSI results have been included here to provide continuity with the previously published results on this measure (Dolan, Warren, & Norton, 1997). A highly significant interaction effect is shown.

The results show highly significant interactions for anxiety, depression, and inwardly and outwardly directed irritability. The mean scores show that in each case this interaction is a result of greater improvement in the admitted group between baseline and one-year follow-up. There is a suggestion of improvement in the non-admitted group for borderline symptoms, anxiety, and depression but of a deterioration in inward and outwardly directed irritability.

The group differences at baseline on anxiety and inward irritability were significant with higher (more pathological) scores in the admitted group. Adjusting for this produced a non-significant interaction for inwardly directed irritability. There was a main effect of time, significant at the $p < .05$ level, however, suggesting that both groups were showing some improvement on this measure.

Table 7.3. Summary of outcomes

	Baseline		One year			
	M	SD	M	SD	F	p
Borderline symptoms						
admitted	34.89	9.39	22.03	15.29	10.85	.001
not admitted	32.98	11.55	28.26	12.90		
Anxiety						
admitted	10.01	2.73	7.61	4.04	11.98	.001
not admitted	8.67	3.07	8.56	3.44		
Depression						
admitted	8.73	3.09	6.70	3.98	4.61	.034
not admitted	7.68	3.78	7.14	3.13		
Inward irritability						
admitted	8.48	3.28	6.25	3.73	7.78	.006
not admitted	6.80	3.53	7.14	3.13		
Outward irritability						
admitted	6.53	2.78	5.77	3.16	5.09	.026
not admitted	6.33	2.87	6.76	3.02		

Confounding variables

When gender and schizoid personality disorder were entered as factors into the individual ANOVAs, no interactions or main effects of these variables were found.

Relationship of outcomes to length of stay in treatment: association of length of stay with follow-up score

Length of stay was negatively correlated with all follow-up scores: the longer a resident stayed in treatment, the lower their follow-up score. These negative correlations were significant to $p < .05$ level with follow-up scores on borderline symptoms, anxiety, depression. The negative correlations with inwardly and outwardly directed irritability were not significant.

Association of length of stay with change

Dolan, Warren, and Norton (1997) found a significant correlation between change in borderline symptoms and length of stay in treatment. These analyses also show a significant correlation between length of stay in treatment and degree of change in depression and anxiety between baseline and one-year post-treatment follow-up. However, there was no significant correlation for inwardly and outwardly directed irritability.

Comparison of change for short-stay and long-stay participants

The admitted patients were therefore divided into long- and short-stay groups. Short-stayers were those who stayed for less than three months, and long-stayers were those who stayed in treatment for nine months or more. The short-stay group stayed in treatment a mean of 34 days (SD = 29.9, range = 2 to 91 days). The long-stay group remained in treatment a mean of 343 days (SD = 32.2, range = 277 to 396 days).

T-tests revealed significant differences for the short- and long-stay groups in change scores for borderline symptoms, anxiety, depression, and inwardly directed irritability. All changes are improvements for the admitted group. Differences in change scores were non-significant for outwardly directed irritability.

Earlier studies (Copas et al., 1984; Dolan, Evans, & Wilson, 1992) had found a significant gender difference in length of stay. This was not evident in this study.

Summary of work in progress

These results augment the existing evidence of positive treatment outcomes. Improvements in core personality disorder pathology previously shown (Dolan, Warren, & Norton, 1997) are supported by the improvements in mood symptomatology shown here. Treatment effects seem to be shown in terms of reductions in anxiety, depression, and outwardly directed irritability, although reduction in inwardly directed irritability would seem to be a weaker effect. It is of interest that there were significant differences between the admitted and non-admitted referrals in terms of anxiety and inwardly directed irritability, on which the admitted group scored more highly. This may suggest a selection effect, which should be explored by future research.

Comment

This prospective outcome study also suffers from some of the methodological shortcomings levelled at previous studies. The use of self-report measures limits the validity of the findings, although some reassurance can be gained from the consistency of effect across multiple self-report measures. The proportion of those about whom we have data at outcome is only a small proportion of the eligible sample in both groups. However, the response rate in this study is not atypical of a personality disorder sample of patients. This limits the generalizability of the findings to personality disorder patients in general. In addition, the follow-up interval differed between the treated and non-treated samples in that the non-treated sample was followed up earlier than were those treated. Alternative study designs, which attempted to match the timing of a non-treated follow-up with a treated follow-up, would only have been possible in theory, since the time spent in treatment for any individual patient could not be known in advance! However, it is also highly unlikely that time alone accounts for such a magnitude of difference between the admitted and non-admitted groups when spontaneous remission in this client group is widely acknowledged to be rare. Further analysis of results using the data collected during treatment may help to substantiate this. The non-admitted comparison group cannot truly be labelled "non-treated", since it is likely that during the study period they had at least some non-specialist treatment that could not be controlled for. The use of this comparison sample is also problematic because the reasons for non-selection or non-attendance may relate to a poorer prognosis at the point of entry to the study. The use of the non-funded group in the study on borderline symptoms, however, provides some reassurance. The non-random allocation to treatment or non-treatment is the most problematic methodological limitation of the study, because this allows systematic variation between groups. Some of the difficulties of applying randomization in this context are identified in the discussion below.

Summary of outcome studies
of Henderson Hospital

Table 7.4 shows a summary of the outcome studies reviewed above. These have shown improvements in those admitted for treatment using a range of approaches to outcome measurement including convictions, psychiatric service usage, and various kinds of psychological functioning. The proportion who improved seems to be consistently around 40%, but this may improve to around 70% for those who stay in treatment for nine months or more. Treatment gains have been shown to be maintained up to five years post-treatment. There is some evidence that a small proportion (3–35%) deteriorate following treatment. Where comparison groups have been used, they have been shown to have fared significantly worse than did those admitted to the treatment, although a small proportion of "untreated" controls did also show improvement over time. Some of the earlier studies were limited in terms of comparison groups, measures used, and follow-up periods, although the methodological approaches can be seen to have evolved over time.

General issues for research in this context

Randomized controlled trials

None of these outcome studies utilized a random allocation to treatment or control group. Randomization is a problematic option for many reasons in this context. In the early life of the Unit, not only were RCTs rare, even in the field of psychopharmacology, but also in other simpler experimental situations in which a clear

Table 7.4. Summary of outcome studies of Henderson Hospital treatment

Study	N	Follow-up period	Criteria of success	Success rate (%)	Description of sample
Rapoport, 1960	64	1 year	improved clinically since admission	41	all discharged men
Tuxford, 1961	86	2 years	in employment	55	all male probation & borstal discharges
			no recidivism	61	
Taylor, 1963	?	9 months	in employment	60	discharged men
Whiteley, 1970	112	2 years	no recidivism	43.6	discharged men
			no re-admission	57.5	
			neither of above	40	
Copas & Whiteley, 1976	104	2 years	no recidivism or re-admission	42	discharged men
	87			47	
	104	5 years	no recidivism or re-admission	33.6	same 104 as above
Copas et al., 1984	194	3 years	no recidivism or re-admission	41	male and female discharges
		5 years	no recidivism or re-admission	36	
	51	3 years	no recidivism or re-admission	23	non-admitted controls
		5 years	no recidivism or re-admission	19	
Dolan, Evans, & Wilson, 1992	62	8 months	improved psychological functioning on SCL–90	55	male and female discharges
Dolan, Warren, Menzies, & Norton, 1996	24	1 year	group cost reduction	by 90	male and female discharges
Dolan, Warren, & Norton, 1997	70	1 year	clinically significant change in borderline personality disorder symptomatology than in untreated controls	42.9	male and female discharges
	67			17.9	male and female non-admitted controls

outcome result could be obtained swiftly—in a matter of days or weeks. However, what is acceptable methodologically has changed since the 1940s and 1950s, and, more recently, the advent of initiatives such as evidence-based medicine (EBM) has increased the profile of RCT evidence for treatments. It is important for this reason to discuss the issues involved in applying RCT methods to therapeutic community treatment.

Residential therapeutic community treatment represents both a complex and a lengthy treatment (average duration seven months), and personality disorder is a complex problem, for which there is no agreed single outcome measure but to which several domains—social, psychological, and penal—are relevant. The length of inpatient treatment of a given patient in the therapeutic community may be up to one year, the nature of the treatment requires a community of up to a maximum of 29, and sustained change post-discharge is needed to provide evidence of an actual treatment effect. Although all RCTs are resource-intensive, an RCT of this treatment would be particularly so, and in previous years funding has not been available to support such a study.

However, in this context there are issues that are more difficult than a lack of finances. The democratic TC, wherein patients treat one another through an exclusively group treatment approach, requires that an adequate population of community members is maintained. From both a clinical and a research perspective this will always remain a central concern. Since any imposed research constraint—such as randomization—could threaten the integrity of the treatment under study if it were to result in inadequate numbers of patients being referred to, or agreeing to be allocated randomly to, the treated sample at a particular point in time.

Some of the strength of this argument against randomization would be lessened were there to be a sufficient and guaranteed excess of referrals over treatment places, such as if the waiting list for admission were sufficiently long. However, this raises two issues: (1) A key feature of this treatment is the process of selecting new residents. The TC requires that patients are involved in the selection of new residents; in fact, the resident group itself has the majority vote in decision-making about the selection of candidates. This requirement increases the resident community's responsibility for the decision to admit an individual, and serves the purpose, for example, of reducing the likelihood of the resident community "washing its hands" of a new resident who turns out to be unpopular and handing over the problem to "staff" who are seen to have imposed this person on the community. In addition, both the community and the new resident have some knowledge of each other before admission—a process that may increase engagement through the candidate's identification with other similar people already receiving treatment in this community. Where there is a waiting list of months' duration, this requirement is decreasingly met, since those who selected the patient are increasingly likely to have themselves left the TC; as a result, the authenticity and power of the treatment is likely to be diminished. (2) This patient group is at high risk of self-damaging behaviour, reconviction for offending, or changes of heart or circumstances, which suggest that opportunities to engage them in treatment should be taken as quickly as possible when they arise. An ethical dilemma is presented by augmenting the waiting list and hence the wait for treatment.

Another difficulty for randomization at the beginning of the referral process arises from selection. While the highly selected nature of the patient group has been levelled as a criticism of the naturalistic research conducted thus far, it is viewed, from a clinical point of view as an essential part of the treatment. The specialist nature of the treatment entails that it is not suitable for all who suffer from the condition, and a schematic process to avoid admitting those who might be damaged is therefore required. For these reasons, randomization would need to occur post-selection. This is likely to have major negative implications for the enhancement of engagement promoted by the selection process as described above.

In the absence of alternative proven effective treatment for people with difficulties this severe, there is a clear ethical obstacle to those who refused to consent to the randomized study conditions to be refused treatment. If there was a "mixture" of randomized and non-randomized, this could pose problems, certainly for the maintenance of "blindness". These are just some of the issues pertinent to RCTs of this treatment, in addition to the other problems with implementing RCTs on long-term treatments for personality disorder with low throughput. As yet, research has not overcome the difficulties posed by the RCT design.

Future directions

From the results of these outcome studies there is a suggestion that the intervention of democratic therapeutic community treatment might be of significant benefit to at least some patients with severe personality disorder. A positive association between length of treatment received and improved outcome has been repeatedly described, although this has not always been statistically significant. When "non-treated" samples have been compared, there has been a consistent finding of significantly greater improvements following this specialist treatment. Future research should broaden the domains in which outcome is measured and look for overall treatment effects. Further consideration should be given to the applicability of the RCT design, and the selection process should be explored further in order to identify more clearly those patients who can be expected to benefit from this treatment and those who cannot.

REFERENCES

Alden, L. E., Wiggins, J. S., & Pincus, A. L. (1990). Construction of circumplex scales for the Inventory of Interpersonal Problems. *Journal of Personality Assessment, 55:* 421–436.

Alexander, F. (1954). Psychoanalysis and psychotherapy. *Journal of the American Psychoanalytic Association, 11:* 722–733.

Alexander, L. B., & Luborsky, L. (1986). The Penn Helping Alliance Scales. In: L. S. Greenberg & W. Pinsof (Eds.), *The Psychotherapeutic Process: A Research Handbook* (pp. 325–366). New York: Guilford Press.

American Psychiatric Association (1994). *Diagnostic and Statistical Manual of Mental Disorders* (4th edition). Washington, DC: APA.

Anderberg, M. (1973). *Cluster Analysis for Applications.* New York: Academic Press.

Antonovsky, A. (1987). *Unraveling the Mystery of Health.* San Francisco, CA: Jossey-Bass.

Arbeitsgruppe OPD (Ed.) (1998). *Operationalisierte Psychodynamische Diagnostik. Grundlagen und Manual.* Bern: Huber.

Bachrach, H. M., Galatzer-Levy, R., Skolnikoff, A., & Waldron, S. (1991). On the efficacy of psychoanalysis. *Journal of the American Psychoanalytic Association, 39:* 871–916.

Basham, R. B. (1986). Scientific and practical advantages of comparative design in psychotherapy research. *Journal of Consulting and Clinical Psychology, 54:* 88–94.

Bateman, A. (1995). The treatment of borderline patients in a day hospital setting. *Psychoanalytic Psychotherapy, 9:* 3–16.

Bateman, A. (1997). Borderline personality disorder and psychotherapeutic psychiatry: An integrative approach. *British Journal of Psychotherapy, 13:* 489–498.

Bateman, A., & Fonagy, P. (1999). The effectiveness of partial hospitalization in the treatment of borderline personality disorder—a randomized controlled trial. *American Journal of Psychiatry, 156*: 1563–1569.

Bateman, A., & Fonagy, P. (2001). Treatment of borderline personality disorder with psychoanalytically oriented partial hospitalization: An 18-month follow-up. *American Journal of Psychiatry, 158*: 36–42.

Beck, A. T., Ward, C. H., Mendelson, M., Mock, J., & Erbaugh, J. (1961). An inventory for measuring depression. *Archives of General Psychiatry, 4*: 561–571.

Becker, P. (1989). *Der Trierer Persönlichkeitsfragebogen TPF*. Göttingen: Hogrefe.

Beckmann, D., Brähler, E., & Richter, H. E. (Eds.) (1990). *Der Giessen-Test (GT): Handbuch* [The Giessen Test: Manual]. Bern: Huber.

Benjamin, L. S. (1974). Structural analysis of social behavior. *Psychological Review, 81*: 395–425.

Beutler, L. E., Machado, P. P., & Neufeldt, S. A. (1994). Therapist variables. In: A. E. Bergin & S. L. Garfield (Eds.), *Handbook of Psychotherapy and Behavior Change*. New York: Wiley.

Bibring, E. (1954). Psychoanalysis and the dynamic psychotherapies. *Journal of the American Psychoanalytic Association, 2*: 745–770.

Bleiberg, E. (1994). Borderline disorders in children and adolescents: The concept, the diagnosis, and the controversies. *Bulletin of the Menninger Clinic, 58*: 169–196.

Blomberg, J., Sandell, R., Lazar, A., & Schubert, J. (1997). *Stability of Effects after Psychotherapy and Psychoanalysis in Terms of Relapse-Rate in the STOPP-Study*. Abstracts of the 28th Annual Meeting, Society for Psychotherapy Research, Geilo, Norway, 25–29 June (p. 67).

Böhle, A., von Wietersheim, J., Wilke, E., & Feiereis, H. (1991). Soziale Integration bei Anorexia nervosa und Bulimie. *Zeitschrift für psychosomatische Medizin und Psychoanalyse, 37*: 282–291.

Brähler, E., & Richter, H. E. (2000). Das psychologische Selbstbild der Deutschen zur Jahrtausendwende [The psychological self-image of Germans in the new millennium]. In: O. Decker & E. Braehler (Eds.), *Deutsche zehn Jahre nach der Wende* (pp. 47–51). Giessen: Psychosozial Verlag.

Bridges, K., & Goldberg, D. (1989). Self-administered scales of neurotic symptoms. In: C. Thompson (Ed.), *The Instruments of Psychiatric Research* (pp. 157–176). New York: Wiley.

Carlsson, A.-M. (1991). Privat psykoterapi finansierad med social-bidrag och bidrag från landstinget: En kartläggning inom Stockholms läns landsting [Psychotherapy in private practice financed with social security or subsidy from the County Council: Mapping within the Stockholm County Council]. *Enheten för Psykosocial Forskning och Utveckling, Rapport 1991:2*, Nacka.

Carlsson, A.-M. (1993). Psykoterapi finansierad med offentliga medel inom Stockholms läns landsting. Kartläggning av organisationen och en utvärdering [Psychotherapy financed with public subsidy within Stockholm County Council: The organisation and an evaluation of the outcome]. *Enheten för Psykosocial Forskning och Utveckling, Rapport 1993:2*, Nacka.

Carroll, L. (1865). *Alice's Adventures in Wonderland*. In: *Complete Illustrated Works of Lewis Carroll* (pp. 11–114). London: Chancellor Press, 1982.

Chambless, D. L., & Hollon, S. D. (1998). Defining empirically supported therapies. *Journal of Clinical and Consulting Psychology, 66*: 7–18.

Chiesa, M., & Fonagy, P. (1999). From the efficacy to the effectiveness model in psychotherapy research: The APP multi-centre project. *Psychoanalytic Psychotherapy, 13*: 259–272.

Cierpka, M., Bucheim, P., Freyberger, H. J., Hoffman, S. O., Janssen, P., Muhs, A., Rudolf, G., Rüger, U., Schneider, W., & Schüssler, G. (1995). Die erste Version einer Operationalisierten Psychodynamischen Diagnostik (OPD–1). *Psychotherapeutics, 40*: 69–78.

Clarkin, J. F., Foelsch, P., Levy, K., Hull, J., Delaney, J., & Kernberg, O. (2001). The development of a psychodynamic treatment for patients with borderline personality disorder: A preliminary study of behavioural change. *Journal of Personality Disorders, 15*: 487–495.

Clarkin, J. F., Kernberg, O. F., & Yeomans, F. (1999). *Transference-Focused Psychotherapy for Borderline Personality Disorder Patients*. New York: Guilford Press.

Cohen, J. (1988). *Statistical Power Analysis for Behavioral Sciences*. Hillsdale, NJ: Lawrence Erlbaum Associates.

Conte, H. R., Plutchik, R., Karasu, T. B., & Vaccaro, E. (1980). A self-report borderline scale: Discriminant validity and preliminary norms. *Journal of Nervous and Mental Disease, 168* (7): 428–435.

Cooke, T., & Campbell, D. (1979). *Quasi-Experimentation*. Boston, MA: Houghton-Mifflin.

Cooper, A. M. (1996). "Psychoanalysis in the 21st Century: Unity in Plurality." Paper presented at the 50th anniversary of the Los Angeles Psychoanalytic Society and Institute, Los Angeles, September.

Copas, J. B., O'Brien, M., Roberts, J. C., & Whiteley, J. S. (1984). Treatment outcome in personality disorder: The effect of social, psychological and behavioural variables. *Personality and Individual Differences, 5*: 565–573.

Copas, J., & Whiteley, J. S. (1976). Predicting success in the treatment of psychopaths. *British Journal of Psychiatry, 129*: 388–392.

Cornwell, J. (1996). *The Power to Harm: Mind, Medicine, and Murder on Trial*. London: Viking.

Dahl, H. (1988). Introduction. In: H. Dahl, H. Kächele, & H. Thomä (Eds.), *Psychoanalytic Process Research Strategies*. Berlin: Springer.

Dancyger, I. F., Sunday, S. R., Eckert, E. D., & Halmi, K. A. (1997). A comparative analysis of Minnesota Multiphasic Personality Inventory profiles of anorexia nervosa at hospital admission, discharge, and 10-year follow up. *Comprehensive Psychiatry, 38*: 185–191.

Davidson, K. M., & Tyrer, P. (1996). Cognitive therapy for antisocial and borderline personality disorders: Single case study series. *British Journal of Clinical Psychology, 35*: 413–429.

Davies-Osterkamp, S., & Kriebel, H. (1993). Konstruktvalidierung von Symptomskalen und Persönlichkeitsstests durch das Inventar zur Erfassung Interpersonal Probleme [Validating constructs of symptom scales and personality tests with the Inventory of Interpersonal Problems]. *Gruppenpsychotherapie und Gruppendynamik, 29*: 295–307.

Davies-Osterkamp, S., Strauss, B., & Schmitz, N. (1996). Interpersonal problems as predictors of symptom-related treatment outcome in long-term psychotherapy. *Psychotherapy Research, 6*: 164–176.

Dawson, D. (1988). Treatment of the borderline patient: Relationship management. *Canadian Journal of Psychiatry, 33*: 370–374.

Deneke, F. W., & Hilgenstock, B. (1989). *Das Narzissmusinventar*. Bern: Huber.

Dennett, D. (1987). *The Intentional Stance*. Cambridge, MA: MIT Press.

Department of Health (1995). *Strategic Report on the Psychotherapies*. London: HMSO.

Department of Health (2001). *Treatment Choice in Psychological Therapies and Counselling*. London: HMSO.

Derogatis, L. R., Lipman, R. S., & Covi, L. (1975). SCL 90: An outpatient psychiatric rating scale. *Psychopharmacology Bulletin, 9*: 13–28.

Derogatis, L. R., Lipman, R. S., Rickels, K., Uhlenhuth, E. H., & Covi, L. (1974). The Hopkins Symptom Checklist (HSCL): A self-report symptom inventory. *Behavioural Science, 19*: 1–15.

Derogatis, L. R., Rickels, K., & Rock, A. F. (1976). The SCL–90 and the MMPI: A step in the validation of a new self-report scale. *British Journal of Psychiatry, 128*: 280–289.

Detre, T., & McDonald, M. C. (1997). Managed care and the future of psychiatry. *Archives of General Psychiatry, 54*: 201–204.

DeWitt, K. N., Hartley, D., Rosenberg, S. E., Zilberg, N. J., & Wallerstein, R. S. (1991). Scales of psychological capacities: Development of an assessment approach. *Psychoanalysis and Contemporary Thought, 14*: 334–343.

DeWitt, K. N., Milbrath, C., & Wallerstein, R. S. (1999). Scales of psychological capacities: Support for a measure of structural change. *Psychoanalysis and Contemporary Thought, 22*: 453–480.

Dilling, H., Mombour, W., & Schmidt, M. H. (1991). *Internationale Klassifikation psychischer Störungen*. Bern: Huber.

Doidge, N. (1997). Empirical evidence for the efficacy of psychoanalytic psychotherapies and psychoanalysis: An overview. *Psychoanalytic Inquiry, 17*: 102–150.

Doidge, N., Simon, B., Gillies, L. A., & Ruskin, R. (1994). Characteristics of psychoanalytic patients under a nationalized health plan: DSM–III–R diagnoses, previous treatment, and childhood trauma. *American Journal of Psychiatry, 151*: 586–590.

Dolan, B., & Coid, J. (1994). *Psychopathic and Antisocial Personality Disorders: Treatment and Research Issues*. London: Gaskell.

Dolan, B., Evans, C., & Norton, K. (1995). Multiple Axis-II diagnosis of personality disorder. *British Journal of Psychiatry, 106*: 107–112.

Dolan, B., Evans, C., & Wilson, J. (1992). Therapeutic community treatment for personality disordered adults: Changes in neurotic symptomatology on follow-up. *International Journal of Social Psychiatry, 38*: 243–250.

Dolan, B., Warren, F., Menzies, D., Norton, K. (1996). Cost-offset following specialist treatment of severe personality disorders. *Psychiatric Bulletin, 20*: 413–417.

Dolan, B., Warren, F., & Norton, K. (1997). Change in borderline symptoms one year after therapeutic community treatment for severe personality disorder. *British Journal of Psychiatry, 171*: 274–279.

Dossmann, R., Kutter, P., Heinzel, R., & Wurmser, L. (1997). The long-term benefits of intensive psychotherapy: A view from Germany. *Psychoanalytic Inquiry (Suppl.)*: 74–86.

Eckert, J., Biermann-Ratjen, E., Brodbeck, D., Burgmeier-Lohse, M., Keller, W., Schulz, E., Schuricht, C., & Strauss, B. (1997). Indikation für Psychotherapie: Welchen Einfluss nehmen interpersonale Probleme des Patienten auf die Indikationsstellung und die Wahl des Settings? [Treatment selection: What influences do interpersonal problems of patients have on the assignment to psychotherapy and the choice of the treatment setting?] *Gruppenpsychotherapie und Gruppendynamik, 33*: 1–17.

Elkin, I., Shea, M. T., Watkins, J. T., Imber, S. D., Sotsky, S. M., Collins, J. F., Glass, D. R., Pilkonis, P. A., Leber, W. R., Docherty, J. P., Fiester, S. J., & Parloff, M. B. (1989). National Institute of Mental Health Treatment of Depression Collaborative Research Program: General effectiveness of treatments. *Archives of General Psychiatry, 46*: 971–982.

Endicott, J., Spitzer, R., Heiss, J., & Cohen, J. (1976). The Global Assessment Scale: A procedure for measuring overall severity of psychiatric disturbance. *Archives of General Psychiatry, 33*: 766–771.

Fahrenberg, J., Hampel, P., & Selg, H. (1989). *Das Freiburger Persönlichkeits-Inventar (FPI–R)*. Göttingen: Hogrefe.

Faulkner, A. (2000). *Strategies for Living: A Report of User-led Research into People's Strategies for Living with Mental Distress*. London: Mental Health Foundation.

Feiereis, H. (1989). *Diagnostik und Therapie der Magersucht und Bulimie*. Munich: Marseille.

Fenichel, O. (1945). *The Psychoanalytic Theory of Neurosis*. New York: Norton.

Fisher, S., & Greenberg, R. P. (1996). *Freud Scientifically Reappraised: Testing the Theories and Therapy*. New York: Wiley.

Fonagy, P. (in press). The development of psychopathology from infancy to adulthood: The mysterious unfolding of disturbance in time. *Infant Mental Health Journal*.

Fonagy, P., Kächele, H., Krause, R., Jones, E., Perron, R., & Lopez, L. (1999). *An Open Door Review of Outcome Studies in Psychoanalysis*. London: UCL.

Fonagy, P., Kennedy, R., Leigh, T., Matton, G., Steele, H., Target, M., & Higgitt, A. (1992). *Attachment, Borderline States and the Representation of Emotions and Cognitions in Self and Other*. Rochester, NY: University of Rochester Press.

Fonagy, P., & Target, M. (1996). Playing with reality: I. Theory of mind and the normal development of psychic reality. *International Journal of Psycho-Analysis, 77*: 217–233.

Fosshage, J. L. (1991). Beyond the basic rule. In: A. Goldberg (Ed.), *The Evolution of Self Psychology, Vol. 7* (pp. 64–71). Hillsdale, NJ: Analytic Press.

Fosshage, J. L. (1997). Psychoanalysis and psychoanalytic psychotherapy: Is there a meaningful distinction in the process? *Psychoanalytic Psychology, 14* (3): 409–425.

Frances, A. J., Fyer, M. R., & Clarkin, J. F. (1986). Personality and suicide. *Annals of the New York Academy of Sciences, 487*: 281–293.

Franke, G. H. (1992). Eine weitere Überprüfung der Symptom-Check-Liste (SCL–90–R) als Forschungsinstrument [A further evaluation of the symptom check list (SCL–90–R) as a research tool]. *Diagnostica, 38*: 160–167.

Freud, S. (1914). Remembering, repeating and working-through (Further recommendations on the technique of psycho-analysis, II). *Standard Edition, 12,* 147.

Fromm-Reichmann, F. (1954). Psychoanalytic and general dynamic conception of theory and therapy: Differences and similarities. *Journal of the American Psychoanalytic Association, 11*: 711–721.

Gabbard, G. O., Gunderson, J. G., & Fonagy, P. (2002). The place of psychoanalytic treatments within psychiatry. *Archives of General Psychiatry, 59:* 505–510.

Gabbard, G. O., Lazar, S. G., Hornberger, J., & Spiegel, D. (1997). The economic impact of psychotherapy: A review. *American Journal of Psychiatry, 154*: 147–155.

Garfield, S. L. (1986). Research on client variables in psychotherapy. In: S. L. Garfield & A. E. Bergin (Eds.), *Handbook of Psychotherapy and Behaviour Change* (3rd edition, pp. 213–256). New York: Wiley.

Garfield, S. L. (1994). Research on client variables in psychotherapy. In: A. E. Bergin & S. L. Garfield (Eds.), *Handbook of Psychotherapy and Behavior Change* (4th edition). New York: Wiley.

Giddens, A. (1999). *Runaway World: How Globalisation Is Reshaping Our Lives.* London: Profile Books.

Gill, M. M. (1954). Psychoanalysis and exploratory frames of psychotherapy. *Journal of the American Psychoanalytic Association, 2*: 771–797.

Gill, M. M. (1984). Psychoanalysis and psychotherapy: A revision. *International Review of Psycho-Analysis, 11*: 161–179.

Gill, M. M. (1988). Converting psychotherapy into psychoanalysis. *Contemporary Psychoanalysis, 24*: 262–274.

Goldfried, M. R. (1995). *From Cognitive-Behavior Therapy to Psychotherapy Integration.* New York: Springer.

Grande, T., Burgmeier-Lohse, M., Cierpka, M., Dahlbender, R. W., Davies-Osterkamp, S., Frevert, G., Joraschky, P., Oberbracht, C., Schauenburg, H., Strack, M., & Strauß, B. (1997). Die Beziehungsachse der Operationalisierten Psychodynamischen Diagnostik (OPD)-Konzept und klinische Anwendungen. *Zeitschrift für psychosomatische Medizin und Psychoanalyse, 43*: 280–296.

Grande, T., & Jakobsen, Th. (1998). Zur Notwendigkeit einer

psychodynamischen Diagnostik und Veränderungsmessung in quantitativen Studien zur analytischen Psychotherapie und Psychoanalyse. In: M. Fäh & G. Fischer (Eds.), *Sinn und Unsinn in der Psychotherapieforschung—Eine kritische Auseinandersetzung mit Aussagen und Forschungsmethoden* (pp. 125–137). Giessen: Psychosozial-Verlag.

Grande, T., Porsch, U., & Rudolf, G. (1988). Muster therapeutischer Zusammenarbeit und ihre Beziehung zum Therapieergebnis. *Zeitschrift für Psychosomatische Medizin und Psychoanalyse, 34*: 76–100.

Grande, T., Rudolf, G., & Oberbracht, C. (1997). Die Praxisstudie Analytische Langzeittherapie. Ein Projekt zur prospektiven Untersuchung struktureller Veränderungen in Psychoanalysen. In: M. Leuzinger-Bohleber & U. Stuhr (Eds.), *Psychoanalysen im Rückblick: Methoden, Ergebnisse und Perspektiven der neueren Katamneseforschung* (pp. 415–431). Giessen: Psychosozial Verlag.

Grande, T., Rudolf, G., & Oberbracht, C. (2000). Veränderungsmessung auf OPD-Basis-Schwierigkeiten und ein neues Konzept. In: W. Schneider & H.-J. Freyberger (Eds.), *Was leistet die OPD* (pp. 148–161). Bern: Huber.

Grande, T., Rudolf, G., Oberbracht, C., & Jakobsen, T. (2001). Therapeutische Veränderungen jenseits der Symptomatik—Wirkungen stationärer Psychotherapie im Licht der Heidelberger Umstrukturierungsskala. *Zeitschrift für Psychosomatische Medizin und Psychotherapie, 47*: 213–233.

Grande, T., Rudolf, G., Oberbracht, C., & Pauli-Magnus, C. (2003). Progressive changes in patients' lives after psychotherapy: Which treatment effects support them? *Psychotherapy Research, 13*: 43–58.

Grawe, K., & Braun, U. (1994). Qualitätskontrolle in der Psychotherapiepraxis. *Zeitschrift für Klinische Psychologie, 23*: 242–267.

Grawe, K., Donati, R., & Bernauer, F. (1994). *Psychotherapie im Wandel: Von der Konfession zur Profession.* Göttingen: Hogrefe.

Gunderson, J. G., Kolb, J. E., & Austin, V. (1981). The diagnostic interview for borderline patients. *American Journal of Psychiatry, 138*: 896–903.

Gunderson, J., & Phillips, K. (1991). A current view of the interface between borderline personality disorder and depression. *American Journal of Psychiatry, 148*: 967–975.

Gurtman, M. B. (1991). Trust, distrust and interpersonal problems: A circumplex analysis. *Journal of Personality and Social Psychology, 62*: 989–1002.

Hamilton, M. (1960). A rating scale for depression. *Journal of Neurology, Neurosurgery and Psychiatry, 23*: 56–62.

Health Council of the Netherlands (2001). *The Efficiency of Long-Term Psychotherapy* (2001/08E). The Hague.

Henderson, D. K. (1939). *Psychopathic States*. London: Chapman & Hall.

Hentschel, U. (1998). *Fragebogen zu Konfliktbewältigungsstrategien*. Göttingen: Hogrefe.

Hertzman, C., & Wiens, M. (1996). Child development and long-term outcomes: A population health perspective and summary of successful interventions. *Social Science and Medicine, 43*: 1083–1095.

Herzog, T., Stiewe, M., Sandholz, A., & Hartmann, A. (1995). Borderline-Syndrom und Essstörungen. Literaturübersicht und Interview-Studie an 172 konsekutiven Inanspruchnahmepatientinnen der Freiburger Essstörungsambulanz. *Psychotherapie, Psychosomatik, Medizinische Psychologie, 45*: 97–108.

Hill, C. E., Helms, J. E., Tichenor, V., Spiegel, S. B., O'Grady, K. E., & Perry, E. S. (1988). Effects of therapist response modes in brief psychotherapy. *Journal of Counselling Psychology, 32*: 3–22.

Hiller, W., Zaudig, M., & Mombour, W. (1995). *Internationale Diagnosen-Checkliste für ICD 10 und DSM IV (IDCL)*. Göttingen: Hogrefe.

Hjelle, L. A., & Ziegler, D. J. (1981). *Personality Theories: Basic Assumptions, Research, and Applications*. New York: McGraw-Hill.

Hoagwood, K., Hibbs, E., Brent, D., & Jensen, P. (1995). Introduction to the special section: Efficacy and effectiveness in studies of child and adolescent psychotherapy. *Journal of Consulting and Clinical Psychology, 63*: 683–687.

Horney, K. (1945). *Our Inner Conflicts*. New York: Norton.

Horowitz, L. M., Rosenberg, S. E., & Bartholomew, K. (1993). Interpersonal problems, attachment styles and outcome in brief dynamic psychotherapy. *Journal of Consulting and Clinical Psychology, 61*: 549–590.

Horowitz, L. M., Rosenberg, S. E., Baer, B. A., Ureno, G., & Villasenor, V. S. (1988). Inventory of Interpersonal Problems: Psychometric properties and clinical applications. *Journal of Clinical and Consulting Psychology, 56*: 885–892.

Horowitz, L. M., Strauss, B., & Kordy, H. (Eds.) (1994). *Manual zum Inventar zur Erfassung für interpersonale Probleme* (IIP–D) [Manual of the Inventory of Interpersonal Problems, German version]. Weinheim: Beltz.

Howard, K. I., Kopta, S. M., Krause, M. S., & Orlinsky, D. E. (1986). The dose–effect relationship in psychotherapy. *American Psychologist*, 41: 159–164.

Huber, D., Henrich, G., & Herschbach, P. (1988). Measuring the quality of life: A comparison between physically and mentally chronically ill patients and healthy persons. *Pharmacopsychiatry*, 21: 453–455.

Huber, D., Henrich, G., & von Rad, M. (2000). Über den Nutzen von Beratungsgesprächen an einer psychosomatisch-psychotherapeutischen Ambulanz. *Psychotherapie Psychosomatik Medizinische Psychologie*, 50: 147–156.

Huber, D., & Klug, G. (1997). "How to Measure Structural Change." Paper presented at the 28th annual meeting of the Society for Psychotherapy Research, Geilo, 25–29 June.

Huber, D., & Klug, G. (1999). The Munich Psychotherapy Study (MPS): Comparing the effects of psychoanalysis and psychotherapy. In: P. Fonagy, H. Kächele, R. Krause, E. Jones, & E. Perron, (Eds.), *An Open Door Review of Outcome Studies in Psychoanalysis*. Report prepared by the Research Committee of the IPA at the request of the President. International Psychoanalytic Association, London <http://www.ipa.org.uk>.

Huber, D., Klug, G., & von Rad, M. (1997). Münchner Psychotherapie-Studie (MPS). In: M. Leuzinger-Bohleber & U. Stuhr (Eds.), *Psychoanalysen im Rückblick*. Gießen: Psychosozial.

Huber, D., Klug, G., & von Rad, M. (2000). Die Münchner Psychotherapiestudie. Ein Vergleich zwischen Psychoanalysen und psychodynamischen Psychotherapien unter besonderer Berücksichtigung therapiespezifischer Ergebnisse. In: U. Stuhr, M. Leuzinger-Bohleber, & M. Beutel (Eds.), *Psychoanalytische Langzeittherapien*. Stuttgart: Kohlhammer.

Hurt, S. W., Brun-Ebérentz, A., Commerford, M. C., Samuel-Lajeuness, B., & Halmi, K. A. (1997). A comparison of psychopathology in eating disorder patients from France and the United States. *International Journal of Eating Disorders*, 22: 153–158.

Hyler, S., Reider, R. O., & Spitzer, R. L. (1987). *Personality Diagnostic Questionnaire—Revised (PDQ–R)*. New York: New York State Psychiatric Institute.

Jacobson, N. S., & Truax, P. (1991). Clinical significance: A statistical approach to defining meaningful change in psychotherapy research. *Journal of Consulting and Clinical Psychology*, 59: 12–19.

Jäger, B., Liedtke, R., Künsebeck, H.-W., Lempa, W., Kersting, A., & Seide, L. (1996). Psychotherapy and bulimia nervosa: Evaluation and long-term follow-up of two conflict-orientated treatment conditions. *Acta Psychiatrica Scandinavica, 93*: 268–278.

Janssen, P. L., Dahlbender, R. W., Freyberger, H. J., Heuft, G., Mans, E. J., Rudolf, G., Schneider, W., & Seidler, G. H. (1996). Leitfaden zur psychodynamisch-diagnostischen Untersuchung. *Psychotherapeutics, 41*: 297–304.

Janssen, P. L., Senf, W., & Meermann, R. (1997). *Klinik der Essstörungen: Magersucht und Bulimie.* Stuttgart: Fischer.

Jensen, P. S., Hibbs, E. D., & Pilkonis, P. A. (1996). From ivory tower to clinical practice: Future directions for child and adolescent psychotherapy research. In: E. D. Hibbs & P. S. Jensen (Eds.), *Psychosocial Treatments for Child and Adolescent Disorders: Empirically Based Strategies for Clinical Practice* (pp. 701–711). Washington, DC: American Psychological Association.

Jones, E. E., Cumming, J. D., & Horowitz, M. J. (1988). Another look at the nonspecific hypothesis of therapeutic effectiveness. *Journal of Consulting and Clinical Psychology, 56*: 48–55.

Jones, M. (1952). *A Study of Therapeutic Communities.* London: Tavistock.

Jöreskog, K. G., & Sörbom, P. (1986). *LISREL VI: Analysis of Linear Structural Relationships by Maximum Likelihood, Instrumental Variables, and Least Square Methods* (4th ed.). Mooresville, IN: Scientific Software.

Kächele, H., & MZ–ESS (1999). Eine multizentrische Studie zu Aufwand und Erfolg bei psychodynamischer Therapie von Essstörugen: Studiendesign und erste Ergebniss. *Psychotherapie, Psychosomatik, Medizinische Psychologie, 49*: 100–108.

Kächele, H., Kordy, H., Richard, M., & Research Group TR-EAT (2001). Therapy amount and outcome of inpatient psychodynamic treatment of eating disorders in Germany: Data from a multicenter study. *Psychotherapy Research, 11*: 239–257.

Kadushin, C. (1969). *Why People Go to Psychiatrists?* New York: Atherton.

Kantrowitz, J. L. (1997). A brief review of psychoanalytic outcome research. *Psychoanalytic Inquiry (Suppl.), 17*: 87–101.

Keller, W., Dilg, R., Westhoff, G., Rohner, R., & Studt, H. H. (1997). Zur Wirksamkeit ambulanter jungianischer Psychoanalysen und Psychotherapien—eine katamnestische Studie. In: M. Leuzinger-Bohleber & U. Stuhr (Eds.), *Psychoanalysen im Rückblick: Methoden, Ergebnisse und Perspektiven der neueren Katamneseforschung* (pp. 432–453). Giessen: Psychosozial Verlag.

Kernberg, O. F. (1991). Psychic structure and structural change: An ego psychology–object relations theory viewpoint. In: T. Shapiro (Ed.), *The Concept of Structure*. Madison, CT: International Universities Press.

Kernberg, O. F. (1999). Psychoanalysis, psychoanalytic psychotherapy and supportive psychotherapy: Contemporary controversies. *International Journal of Psycho-Analysis, 30* (6): 1075–1091.

Kiresuk, T. J., & Sherman, R. E. (1968). GAS: A general method for evaluating comprehensive community mental health programs. *Community Mental Health Journal, 4*: 443–453.

Kline, R. B. (1998). *Principles and Practice of Structural Equation Modeling*. New York: Guilford Press.

Knapp, M. R. J. (1997). Economic evaluations and interventions for children and adolescents with mental health problems. *Journal of Child Psychology and Psychiatry, 38* (1): 3–25.

Lambert, M. J., & Hill, C. E. (1994). Assessing psychotherapy outcomes and processes. In: A. E. Bergin & S. L. Garfield (Eds.), *Handbook of Psychotherapy and Behaviour Change*. New York: Wiley.

Linehan, M. M. (1993a). *Cognitive-Behavioural Treatment of Borderline Personality Disorder*. New York: Guilford Press.

Linehan, M. M. (1993b). *The Skills Training Manual for Treating Borderline Personality Disorder*. New York: Guilford Press.

Linehan, M. M., Armstrong, H. E., Suarez, A., Allman, D., & Heard, H. (1991). Cognitive-behavioural treatment of chronically parasuicidal borderline patients. *Archives of General Psychiatry, 48*: 1060–1064.

Lubin, B., Hornstra, R. K., Lewis, R. V., & Bechtel, B. S. (1973). Correlates of initial treatment assignment in a community mental health center. *Archives of General Psychiatry, 29*: 497–504.

Luborsky, L., Diguer, L., Luborsky, E., Singer, B., Dickter, D., & Schmidt, K. A. (1993). The efficacy of dynamic psychotherapies: Is it true that "Everyone has won and all must have prizes"? In: N. E. Miller, L. Luborsky, J. P. Barber, & J. P. Docherty (Eds.), *Psychodynamic Treatment Research*. New York: Basic Books.

Luborsky, L., Diguer, L., Seligman, D. A., Rosenthal, R., Krause, E. D., Johnson, S., Halperin, G., Bishop, M., Berman, J. S., & Schweizer, E. (1999). The researcher's own therapy allegiances: A "wild card" in comparisons of treatment efficacy. *Clinical Psychology: Science and Practice, 6*: 96–132.

Main, T. F. (1946). The hospital as a therapeutic institution. *Bulletin of the Menninger Clinic, 10*: 66–68.

Main, T. F. (1957). The ailment. *British Journal of Medical Psychology, 30*: 129–145.

Main, T. F. (1983). The concept of the therapeutic community: Its variations and vicissitudes. In: M. Pines, *The Evolution of Group Analysis*. London: Routledge & Kegan Paul.

Manning, N., & Rapoport, R. (1976). Rejection and reincorporation: A case study in social research utilisation. *Social Science and Medicine, 10*: 459–468.

Markowitz, J. C., & Street, L. L. (1999). NIMH propels psychotherapy on a new course. *Psychiatric News*, 15 October.

Marziali, E., Newman, T., Munroe-Blum, H., & Dawson, D. (1989). "Manual and Training Materials for Relationship Management Psychotherapy." Unpublished manuscript.

Mayes, N., & Pope, C. (2000). Qualitative research in health care: Assessing quality and qualitative research. *British Medical Journal, 320*: 50–52.

Menninger, K., Mayman, M., & Pruyser, P. (1963). *The Vital Balance: The Life Process in Mental Health and Illness*. New York: Viking Press.

Menzies, D., Dolan, B. M., & Norton, K. (1993). Are short term savings worth long term costs? Funding psychotherapeutic inpatient treatment for personality disorders. *Psychiatric Bulletin, 17*: 517–519.

Mercer, R. C., & Loesch, L. C. (1979). Audiotape ratings: Comments and guidelines. *Psychotherapy: Theory, Research and Practice, 16*: 79–85.

Michels, R. (1994). Psychoanalysis enters its second century. *Annual of Psychoanalysis, 22*: 37–45.

Mohr, D. C., Beutler, L. E., Engle, D., Shoham-Salomon, V., Bergan, J., Kaszniak, A. W., & Yost, E. B. (1990). Identification of patients at risk for nonresponse and negative outcome in psychotherapy. *Journal of Consulting and Clinical Psychology, 58*: 622–628.

Moore, B. E., & Fine, B. D. (1990). *Psychoanalytic Terms & Concepts*. New Haven, CT: Yale University Press.

Muhs, A. (1993). Results from the psychosomatic hospital Mannheim. *Gruppenpsychotherapie und Gruppendynamik, 29*: 259–270.

Norton, K. (1992a). A culture of enquiry—its preservation or loss. *International Journal of Therapeutic Communities, 13* (1): 3–26.

Norton, K. (1992b). Personality disordered individuals: The Henderson Hospital model of treatment. *Criminal Behaviour and Mental Health, 2*: 180–191.

Norton, K. (1995). Personality disordered forensic patients and the therapeutic community. In: C. Cordess & M. Cox (Eds.), *Forensic Psychotherapy*. London: Jessica Kingsley.

Norton, K. (1996). How therapeutic communities work. In: G. Edwards & C. Dare (Eds.), *Psychotherapy Psychological Treatment and the Addictions*. Cambridge: Cambridge University Press.

Norton, K., & Dolan, B. (1995a). Acting out and the institutional response. *Journal of Forensic Psychiatry, 6* (2): 317–332.

Norton, K., & Dolan, B. (1995b). Assessing change in personality disorder. *Current Opinions in Psychiatry, 8*: 371–375.

Norton, K., & Hinshelwood, R. D. (1996). Severe personality disorder: Treatment issues and selection for in-patient psychotherapy. *British Journal of Psychiatry, 168*: 723–731.

O'Connor, T., Bredenkamp, D., Rutter, M., & the English and Romanian Adoptees Study Team (1999). Attachment disturbances and disorders in children exposed to early severe deprivation. *Infant Mental Health Journal, 20*: 10–29.

O'Connor, T., Rutter, M., & the English and Romanian Adoptees Study Team (2000). Attachment disorder behavior following early severe deprivation: Extension and longitudinal follow-up. *Journal of the American Academy of Child and Adolescent Psychiatry, 39* (June): 703–712.

Olfson, M., & Pincus, H. A. (1994a). Psychotherapy in the United States, I: Volume, costs, and user characteristics. *American Journal of Psychiatry, 151*: 1281–1288.

Olfson, M., & Pincus, H. A. (1994b). Psychotherapy in the United States, II: Patterns of utilization. *American Journal of Psychiatry, 151*: 1289–1294.

OPD-Task Force (Eds.) (2001). *Operationalized Psychodynamic Diagnostics. Foundations and Manual*. Seattle, Toronto, Göttingen: Hogrefe & Huber.

Pfeffer, A. Z. (1959). A procedure for evaluating the results of psychoanalysis: A preliminary report. *Journal of the American Psychoanalytic Association, 7*: 418–444.

Piaget, J. (1970). *Structuralism*. New York: Basic Books.

Pulver, S. E. (1991). Psychic structure, function, process, and content: Toward a definition. In: T. Shapiro (Ed.), *The Concept of Structure*. Madison, CT: International Universities Press.

Rangell, L. (1954). Similarities and differences between psychoanalysis and dynamic psychotherapy. *Journal of the American Psychoanalytic Association, 2*: 734–744.

Rapoport, R. (1960). *The Community as Doctor*. London: Tavistock.

Robinson, L. A., Berman, J. S., & Neimeyer, R. A. (1990). Psychotherapy for the treatment of depression: A comprehensive review of controlled outcome research. *Psychological Bulletin, 108*: 30–39.

Rose, D. (2001). *User's Voices: The Perspective of Mental Health Service Users on Community and Hospital Care.* London: Sainsbury Centre for Mental Health.

Rosenberg, M. (1965). *The Measurement of Self-Esteem.* Princeton, NJ: Princeton University Press.

Rosenbluth, M. (1991). New uses of countertransference for the inpatient treatment of borderline personality disorder. *Canadian Journal of Psychiatry, 36*: 280–284.

Rosenvinge, J. H., & Mouland, S. O. (1990). Outcome and prognosis of anorexia nervosa: A retrospective study of 41 subjects. *British Journal of Psychiatry, 156*: 92–97.

Rosser, R., Birch, S., Bond, H., Denford, J., & Schacter, J. (1987). Five year follow-up of patients treated with in-patient psychotherapy at the Cassel Hospital for Nervous Diseases. *Journal of the Royal Society of Medicine, 80*: 549–555.

Roth, A., & Fonagy, P. (1996). *What Works for Whom? A Critical Review of Psychotherapy Research.* New York: Guilford Press.

Roth, A., Fonagy, P., & Parry, G. (1996). Psychotherapy research, funding, and evidence-based practice. In: A. Roth & P. Fonagy (Eds.), *What Works for Whom? A Critical Review of Psychotherapy Research* (pp. 37–56). New York: Guilford Press.

Rudolf, G. (1991a). *Die therapeutische Arbeitsbeziehung. Untersuchungen zum Zustandekommen, Verlauf und Ergebnis analytischer Psychotherapien. Unter Mitarbeit von T. Grande und U. Porsch.* Berlin: Springer.

Rudolf, G. (1991b). PSKB–Se—ein psychoanalytisch fundiertes Instrument zur Patienten-Selbsteinschätzung. *Zeitschrift für Psychosomatische Medizin und Psychoanalyse, 37*: 350–360.

Rudolf, G., & Grande, T. (1997). "Praxisstudie Analytische Langzeittherapie. Forschungsprojekt zur Untersuchung der Effektivität und Effizienz höherfrequenter analytischer Langzeitpsychotherapien." Projektantrag.

Rudolf, G., Grande, T., Oberbracht, C. (2000). Die Heidelberger Umstrukturierungsskala: Ein Modell der Veränderung in psychoanalytischen Therapien und seine Operationalisierung in einer Schätzskala. *Psychotherapeutics, 45*: 237–246.

Rudolf, G., Grande, T., Oberbracht, C., & Jakobsen, T. (1996). Erste empirische Untersuchungen zu einem neuen diagnostischen System: Die Operationalisierte Psychodynamische Diagnostik (OPD). *Zeitschrift für Psychosomatische Medizin und Psychoanalyse, 42*: 343–357.

Rudolf, G., Laszig, P., & Henningsen, P. (1997). Dokumentation im Dienste von klinischer Forschung und Qualitätssicherung. *Psychotherapeutics, 42*: 145–155.

Rudolf, G., Oberbracht, C., & Grande, T. (1998). Die Struktur-Checkliste. Ein anwenderfreundliches Hilfsmittel für die Strukturdiagnostik nach OPD. In: H. Schauenburg, H. J. Freyberger, M. Cierpka, & P. Buchheim (Eds.), *OPD in der Praxis. Konzepte, Anwendungen, Ergebnisse der Operationalisierten Psychodynamischen Diagnostik* (pp. 167–181). Bern: Huber.

Rutter, M. (2000). Psychosocial influences: Critiques, findings and research needs. *Development and Psychopathology, 12*: 375–405.

Ryle, A. (1997). *Cognitive Analytic Therapy and Borderline Personality Disorder: The Model and the Method.* Chichester: Wiley.

Sackett, D. L., Rosenberg, W. M., Gray, J. A. M., Haynes, R. B., & Richardson, W. S. (1996). Evidence based medicine: What it is and what it isn't. *British Medical Journal, 312*: 71–72.

Sandell, R., Blomberg, J., & Lazar, A. (1999). Wiederholte Langzeitkatamnesen von Langzeitpsychotherapien und Psychoanalysen. *Zeitschrift für Psychosomatische Medizin und Psychotherapie, 45*: 43–56.

Sandell, R., Blomberg, J., & Lazar, A. (2002). Time matters: On temporal interactions in psychoanalysis and long-term psychotherapy. *Psychotherapy Research, 12*: 39–58.

Schepank, H. (1995). *BSS—Der Beeinträchtigungs-Schwere-Score.* Göttingen: Beltz-Test.

Schork, E. J., Eckert, E. D., & Halmi, K. A. (1994): The relationship between psychopathology, eating disorder diagnosis, and clinical outcome at 10-year follow-up in anorexia nervosa. *Comprehensive Psychiatry, 35*: 113–123.

Schubert, J., & Blomberg, J. (1994). Psykoterapipatienter i offentlig vård. En social, demografisk och diagnostisk undersökning [Psychotherapy patients in public health care: A social, demographic and diagnostic study]. *Rapporter från PI, 7.* Stockholms läns landstings Psykoterapiinstitut.

Schulte, D. (1995). How treatment success could be assessed. *Psychotherapy Research, 5* (4): 281–296.

Seligman, M. E. P. (1995). The effectiveness of psychotherapy: The Consumer Reports study. *American Psychologist, 50*: 965–974.

Senf, W. (1989). Psychoanalytische Betrachtungen zur Bulimie. In: A.

Kämmerer & B. Klingenspor (Eds.), *Bulimie—Zum Verständnis einer geschlechtsspezifischen Erkrankung* (pp. 88–103). Stuttgart: Kohlhammer.

Shaffer, D., Gould, M. S., Brasic, J., Ambrosini, P., Fisher, P., Bird, H., & Aluwahlia, S. (1983). A children's global assessment scale (CGAS). *Archives of General Psychiatry, 40*: 1228–1231.

Shapiro, D., Rees, A., Barkham, M., Hardy, G., Reynolds, S., & Startup, M. (1995). Effects of treatment duration and severity of depression on the maintenance of gains after cognitive-behavioral and psychodynamic-interpersonal psychotherapy. *Journal of Consulting and Clinical Psychology, 63*: 378–387.

Shapiro, D. A., & Shapiro, D. (1982). Meta-analysis of comparative therapy outcome studies: A replication and refinement. *Psychological Bulletin, 92*: 581–604.

Shea, M. T., Elkin, I., Imber, S. D., Sotsky, S. M., Watkins, J. T., Collins, J. F., Pilkonis, P. A., Beckham, E., Glass, D. R., Dolan, R. T., & Parloff, M. B. (1992). Course of depressive symptoms over followup: Findings from the NIMH treatment of depression collaborative research programme. *Archives of General Psychiatry, 49*: 782–787.

Shea, M. T., Pilkonis, P. A., Beckham, E., Collins, J. F., Elkin, I., Sotsky, S. M., & Docherty, J. P. (1990). Personality disorders and treatment outcome in the NIMH Treatment of Depression Collaborative Research Program. *American Journal of Psychiatry, 147*: 711–718.

Shrout, P. E., & Fleiss, J. L. (1979). Intraclass correlations: Uses in assessing rater-reliability. *Psychological Bulletin, 86*: 420–428.

Smith, M. L., Glass, G. V., & Miller, T. I. (1980). *The Benefits of Psychotherapy*. Baltimore, MD: Johns Hopkins University Press.

Snaith, R. P., Constantopoulos, A. A., Jardine, M. Y., & McGuffin, P. (1978). A clinical scale for the self assessment of irritability. *British Journal of Psychiatry, 132*: 164–171.

Solms, M. (2000). Dreaming and REM sleeping are controlled by different brain mechanisms. *Behavior and Brain Sciences, 23*: 843–850, 904–1121.

Solms, M., & Nersessian, E. (1999). Freud's theory of affect. *Neuro-Psychoanalysis, 1*: 5–14.

Sommer, G., & Fydrich, T. (1991). Entwicklung und Überprüfung eines Fragebogens zur Sozialen Unterstützung (F–SOZU). *Diagnostica, 37*: 160–178.

Spitzer, R. L., Williams, J. B., Gibbon, M., & First, M. B. (1990). *User's Guide for the Structured Clinical Interview for DSM–III–R*. Washington, DC: American Psychiatric Association.

Stevenson, J., & Meares, R. (1992). An outcome study of psychotherapy for patients with borderline personality disorder. *American Journal of Psychiatry, 149*: 358–362.

Stevenson, J., & Meares, R. (1995). Borderline patients at 5 year follow-up. *Proceedings of Annual Congress of the Royal Australian and New Zealand College of Psychiatrists.* Cairns, Australia.

Stevenson, J., & Meares, R. (1999). Psychotherapy with borderline patients: II. A preliminary cost benefit study. *Australian and New Zealand Journal of Psychiatry, 33*: 473–477.

Stiles, W. B., Meshot, C. M., Anderson, T. M., & Sloan, W. W. (1992). Assimilation of problematic experiences: The case of John Jones. *Psychotherapy Research, 2*: 81–101.

Strauss, B. (1992). Empirische Untersuchungen zur stationären Gruppenpsychotherapie [Empirical studies on inpatient group psychotherapy]. *Gruppenpsychotherapie und Gruppendynamik, 28*: 125–149.

Strauss, B., & Burgmeier-Lohse, M. (1993). Ergebnisse aus der Klinik für Psychotherapie Kiel [Results from the University Hospital Kiel]. *Gruppenpsychotherapie und Gruppendynamik, 29*: 237–244.

Strauss, B., & Burgmeier-Lohse, M. (1994). *Stationäre Langzeitgruppenpsychotherapie* [Long-term group inpatient psychotherapy]. Heidelberg: Asanger.

Strauss, B., & Burgmeier-Lohse, M. (1995). Merkmale der Passung zwischen Therapeut und Patient als Determinante des Behandlungsergebnisses in der stationären Gruppenpsychotherapie [Characteristics of the patient treatment fit as a determinant of treatment oucome in inpatient group psychotherapy]. *Zeitschrift für Psychosomatische Medizin und Psychoanalyse, 41*: 127–140.

Strauss, B., Eckert, J., & Hess, H. (1993). Integration und Diskussion der Ergebnisse [Integration and discussion of the results]. *Gruppenpsychotherapie und Gruppendynamik, 29*: 286–294.

Strauss, B., Eckert, J., & Ott, J. (Eds.) (1993). Interpersonale Probleme in der stationären Gruppenpsychotherapie—Themenheft [Interpersonal problems in inpatient psychotherapy—Special issue]. *Gruppenpsychotherapie und Gruppendynamik, 29* (3): 223–323.

Strauss, B., & Kächele, H. (1998). The writing on the wall: Comments on the current discussion about empirically validated treatments in Germany. *Psychotherapy Research, 8*: 158–170.

Strauss, B., Kriebel, R., & Mattke, D. (1998). Probleme der Qualitätssicherung in der stationären Gruppenpsychotherapie [Problems of quality assurance in inpatient group psychotherapy]. *Psychotherapeut, 43*: 18–25.

Strauss, B., Lobo-Drost, A., & Pilkonis, P. A. (1999). Einschätzung von Bindungsstilen bei Erwachsenen—Erste Erfahrungen mit der deutschen Version einer Prototypenbeurteilung [Assessment of attachment styles in adults—First experiences with the German version of a prototype rating]. *Zeitschrift für Klinische Psychologie, Psychiatrie und Psychotherapie, 47*: 347–364.

Strupp, H. H., Horowitz, L. M., & Lambert, M. J. (Eds.) (1997). *Measuring Patient Changes.* Washington, DC: American Psychological Association.

Strupp, H. H., Schacht, T. E., & Henry, W. P. (1988). Problem–treatment–outcome congruence: A principle whose time has come. In: H. Dahl, H. Kächele, & H. Thomä (Eds.), *Psychoanalytic Process Research Strategies* (pp. 1–14). Berlin: Springer-Verlag.

Stuhr, E. (Ed.) (1997). *Therapieerfolg als Prozess—Leitlinien für eine künftige Psychotherapieforschung* [Therapeutic success as process: Guidelines for future psychotherapy research]. Heidelberg: Asanger.

Taylor, F. H. (1963). The treatment of delinquent psychopaths. *The Howard Journal, 1*: 1–9.

Taylor, L., Adelman, H., & Kayser-Boyd, N. (1986). The Origin Climate Questionnaire as a tool for studying psychotherapeutic process. *Journal of Child and Adolescent Psychotherapy, 3*: 10–16.

Thiel, A., Züger, M., Jacoby, G. E., & Schüßler, G. (1999). Welche Bedeutung haben narzißtische Selbst-Störungen für die Prognose der Anorexia und Bulimia nervosa? Eine prospektive Katamnese über 30 Monate. *Zeitschrift für psychosomatische Medizin und Psychoanalyse, 45*: 57–76.

Tress, W. (Ed.) (1993). *SASB—Die Strukturale Analyse Sozialen Verhaltens.* Heidelberg: Asanger.

Tschuschke, V. (1993). *Wirkfaktoren stationärer Gruppenpsychotherapie* [Therapeutic factors of inpatient group psychotherapy]. Göttingen: Vandenhoek & Ruprecht.

Tuxford, J. (1961). *Treatment as a Circular Process.* London: King Edward's Hospital Fund.

Tyrer, P., & Johnson, T. (1996). Establishing the severity of personality disorder. *American Journal of Psychiatry, 153* (12): 1593–1597.

Tyrer, P., Seivewright, N., Ferguson, B., et al. (1990). The Nottingham Study of Neurotic Disorder: Relationship between personality status and symptoms. *Psychological Medicine, 20*: 423–431.

Vaughan, S. C., Marshall, R. D., MacKinnon, R. A., Vaughan, R., Mellman, L., & Roose, S. P. (2000). Can we do psychoanalytic outcome research? A feasibility study. *International Journal of Psycho-Analysis, 81*: 513–527.

Vessey, J., & Howard, K. (1993). Who seeks psychotherapy? *Psychotherapy, 30*: 546–553.

von Rad, M., Senf, W., & Bräutigam, W. (1998). Psychotherapie und Psychoanalyse in der Krankenversorgung: Ergebnisse des Heidelberger Katamneseprojekts [Psychotherapie and psychoanalysis in the health system: Results of the Heidelberg follow-up study]. *Psychotherapie, Psychosomatik, Medizinische Psychologie, 48*: 88–100.

Waldinger, R. J., & Gunderson, J. G. (1984). Completed therapies with borderline patients. *American Journal of Psychotherapy, 38*: 190–202.

Wallerstein, R. S. (1986). *Forty-two Lives in Treatment*. New York: Guilford Press.

Wallerstein, R. S. (1989). The psychotherapy research project of the Menninger Foundation: An overview. *Journal of Consulting and Clinical Psychology, 57*: 195–205.

Wallerstein, R. S. (1991). Assessment of structural change in psychoanalytic therapy and research. In: T. Shapiro (Ed.), *The Concept of Structure in Psychoanalysis*. Madison, CT: International Universities Press.

Wallerstein, R. S. (n.d.). "The Scales of Psychological Capacities, Version 1." Unpublished manuscript.

Weber, J., Solomon, M., & Bachrach, H. (1985). Characteristics of psychoanalytic clinic patients: Report of the Columbia psychoanalytic centre research project (I). *International Review of Psycho-Analysis, 12*: 13–26.

Weissman, M. M., & Bothwell, S. (1976). Assessment of social adjustment by patient self-report. *Archives of General Psychiatry, 33*: 1111–1115.

Weisz, J. R., Donenberg, G. R., Han, S. S., Weiss, B., et al. (1995). Bridging the gap between laboratory and clinic in child and adolescent psychotherapy. *Journal of Consulting and Clinical Psychology, 63*: 688–701.

Weisz, J. R., Hawley, K. M., Pilkonis, P. A., Woody, S. R., & Follette, W. C. (2000). Stressing the (other) three Rs in the search for empirically supported treatments: Review procedures, research quality, relevance to practice and the public interest. *Clinical Psychology: Science and Practice, 7* (3): 243–258.

Weisz, J. R., & Jensen, P. S. (1999). Efficacy and effectiveness of child and adolescent psychotherapy and pharmacotherapy. *Mental Health Services Research, 1*: 125–157.

Wells, K. B. (1999). Treatment research at the crossroads: The scientific interface of clinical trials and effectiveness research. *American Journal of Psychiatry, 156*: 5–10.

Westen, D., & Morrison, K. (2001). A multidimensional meta-analysis of treatments for depression, panic, and generalized anxiety disorder: An empirical examination of the status of empirically supported therapies. *Journal of Consulting and Clinical Psychology, 69* (6): 875–899.

Whiteley, J. S. (1970). The response of psychopaths to a therapeutic community. *British Journal of Psychiatry, 116* (534): 517–529.

Whiteley, J. S. (1980). The Henderson Hospital: A community study. *International Journal of Therapeutic Communities, 1* (2): 38–58.

Whiteley, J. S. (1986). Sociotherapy and psychotherapy in the treatment of personality disorder. Discussion paper. *Journal of the Royal Society of Medicine, 79*: 721–725.

Wiggins, J. S., Phillips, N., & Trapnell, P. (1989). Circular reasoning about interpersonal behaviour: Evidence concerning some untested assumptions underlying diagnostic classification. *Journal of Personality and Social Psychology, 56*: 296–305.

Wing, J., Curtis, R., & Beevor, A. (1996). *HONOS: Health of the Nation Outcome Scales—A Report on Research and Development (July 1993–December 1995)*. London: College Research Unit, Royal College of Psychiatrists.

Wing, J., Lelliott, P., & Beevor, A. S. (2000). Progress on HoNOS. *British Journal of Psychiatry, 176*: 392–393.

Zielke, M., & Kopf-Mehnert, C. (1978). *Veränderungsfragebogen des Erlebens und Verhaltens, VEV*. Weinheim: Beltz.

Zimmermann, M. (1994). Diagnosing personality disorders. *Archives of General Psychiatry, 51*: 225–245.

INDEX